Crying in the Shower

Jill Lien

Crying in the Shower

Jill Lien

ISBN: 979-8-9916699-3-1

For the women who keep going, even when no one sees how hard it is.

For my daughters, Kate and Sam, and for Jen, because the "in-law" part never really fit.

I have watched each of you face difficult seasons and keep going.

You have carried more than your share, doubted yourselves, and kept showing up for the people who needed you.

You remind me that strength isn't about having an easy life.

It's about continuing anyway.

This book is for every woman who has ever stood under running water trying to gather herself before going back out into the world.

Especially you three.

Love,

Mum

Table of Contents

PART ONE

Turning on the Tap
Where Overwhelm Begins to Have a Name

Chapter One

Behind the Bathroom Door

The place where strong women finally let themselves fall apart.

Steam fills the bathroom. The door is locked. The water runs louder than it needs to.

And somewhere in the middle of it—where no one can see and no one can hear—a woman is crying.

Not because she is weak.
Not because she cannot cope.
But because she has been coping for far too long.

The shower is often the only place it can happen. The only place where the noise of running water hides the sound of tears. The only place where, for a few minutes, the mask can come off.

It was a Tuesday. Or maybe a Wednesday—honestly, the days had started to blur together in that way they do when you're running on fumes and calling it fine. I was standing in my shower, water turned up hotter than was sensible, and I was crying. Not the elegant, single-tear-rolling-down-the-cheek kind of crying you see in films. The ugly kind. The kind where your face crumples and your shoulders shake, and you're grateful for the sound of the water because at least no one can hear you.

What had tipped me over? I couldn't even tell you precisely. It wasn't one thing—it was *everything.* Seven months earlier, my husband and I had left Wyoming—a place we'd lived for six years, where we'd built friendships and community and a life we loved—and moved to Kentucky. The reasons were practical: better healthcare access for my husband, whose health was changing in ways that needed more specialist support, and an airport in Nashville that flies direct to England, making it easier to see my daughters. Good reasons. The right reasons, probably. But standing in that shower, I missed Wyoming with an ache that surprised me. I missed our friends there, the ones who knew our history, who didn't need everything explained.

Here's the thing about starting over: you can't make new old friends. You can make new friends—and I have, a few—but those relationships take time to deepen. Years. And in the meantime, there's a particular loneliness that comes from being surrounded by people who don't really know you yet, who see the professional, competent version you present to the world, not the woman crying in the shower.

And I *couldn't* show them that woman. That's the bitter irony of my work: I'm supposed to be the strong one. People come to me when they're struggling, when they need help finding their way through. I'm the professional, the expert, the one with the tools. How could I admit that I was falling apart myself? So I didn't. I kept the mask firmly in place and saved the breaking for the bathroom.

We'd bought a "doer-upper" that, it turned out, wouldn't do itself up. The roof was pouring water into the center of the house when we arrived, so that had to be fixed immediately, and the list of what still needed doing seemed to grow rather than shrink. I was building my business from scratch in a community that didn't know me—not just for the income, though yes, I need to provide for my family—but because helping people is who I am. It's what gets me out of bed. I was doing the radio shows and newspaper columns and training courses and conference talks because I genuinely wanted to make a difference here, to build something meaningful.

And somewhere underneath all that drive was something I perhaps hadn't wanted to look at too closely: at sixty-seven, I'm struggling in ways I simply didn't when I was younger. The resilience that used to come naturally now requires effort. The energy I once took for granted has to be carefully managed. I have a cancer diagnosis I'm navigating, with appointments and treatments woven into already full days. And there was a stalker—yes, really—who had taken to watching me from my back garden in the dark, turning my home into something that no longer felt entirely safe.

And through all this, the thought that kept circling, *I should be able to handle this.*

That thought—that lie I'd been telling myself—it just broke open in the steam. And I stood there, water pounding my shoulders, and I let myself fall apart for a few minutes. Because the bathroom was the only place I could.

Maybe, I thought afterwards, I'd been hiding behind the busyness. Throwing myself into work and projects and endless to-do lists because it felt better than sitting still and confronting the truth: that this season of life was harder than I'd expected. That I was tired in a way I couldn't quite explain. That somewhere along the line, I'd stopped putting myself on my own list of people to take care of.

Here's the thing, though. Even in that moment—mascara running, nose streaming, looking absolutely nothing like the competent professional I present to the world—a thought surfaced. Not a comforting thought, exactly. More of a recognition.

I am not the only woman standing in her shower right now, crying where no one can see her.

I thought about the young mother down the road, the one with the toddler and the newborn and the dark circles she tries to hide with concealer. I thought about my friend who's caring for her elderly father while holding down a demanding job and a marriage that's fraying at the edges. I thought about the executive women I've worked with over the years, the ones with the impressive titles and the corner offices, who confess in quiet moments that they're barely keeping their heads above water. The sandwich generation, pressed between children who need them and parents who need them, wondering who exactly is supposed to be taking care of *them.* The women who've moved far from home and left their people behind. The women whose bodies or circumstances have changed and who are quietly grieving the version of themselves they used to be. The therapists and nurses and carers and mothers who spend all day being strong for everyone else and have nothing left for themselves.

All of us, crying in our showers. All of us, thinking we're the only ones who can't cope.

And standing there, water going lukewarm, I thought: *Someone should write a book about this.*

Then I thought: *Oh. I suppose that someone might be me.*

So here we are, you and I. I don't know what brought you to this book. Maybe you saw the title and something in you went *yes*—that immediate, gut-level recognition that needs no explanation. Maybe someone who loves you thought you might need it. Maybe you're not even sure why you picked it up, only that something felt heavy lately and you were looking for... something. Permission, perhaps. Or just proof that you're not losing your mind.

Whatever brought you here, I want you to know something before we go any further:

You are not weak. You are not failing. You are not the only one.

The fact that you're struggling doesn't mean you're broken. It means you're human, carrying more than any one person should reasonably carry, in a world that has somehow convinced women that we should be able to do it all, have it all, and look serene while doing it.

That's not strength. That's a lie we've been sold. And I think it's time we stopped buying it.

SHE CRIED TOO

Arianna Huffington

"I had bought into the collective delusion that in order to be the super-founder and super mom of two teenage daughters, I didn't have time to take care of myself. So I collapsed and broke my cheekbone on the way down."

Arianna Huffington was two years into building *The Huffington Post*—one of the most successful media ventures of its time—when her body simply gave out. She collapsed from exhaustion in her home office, hit her head on her desk, and woke up in a pool of blood. The diagnosis? Burnout. She went on to build an entire company dedicated to helping others avoid the same fate, but she had to break first. Even the most successful among us have cried—or collapsed—behind closed doors.

The shower, it turns out, is significant. It's not just a random location for a breakdown—it's often the *only* location available.

Think about it. When you're a mother, the bathroom is the sole room in the house where a locked door is even vaguely acceptable (and even then, small fingers often appear underneath it, accompanied by urgent questions about snacks). When you're a caregiver, it's the one place you can step away without someone immediately needing you. When you're holding it together at work, it's the refuge between meetings where you can press your palms against the cool tiles and breathe. And when you're the person everyone else comes to for support? It might be the only space where you're allowed to need something yourself.

The shower itself offers practical benefits for falling apart. The running water masks the sound of crying. The steam explains away red eyes. The door is locked. You're alone—perhaps for the only five minutes you'll be alone all day. And there's something about the water itself, isn't there? The way it runs over you, washing away what you can't carry anymore, even if only temporarily.

Women have been crying in showers for as long as there have been showers. Before that, we cried in outhouses and behind haystacks and in whatever private corner we could find. We've always needed a place to put down the mask. What's changed isn't the crying—it's the weight of what we're carrying.

Let me be clear about what this book is and isn't.

This is not a book that will tell you to take more bubble baths. (Though if bubble baths help, by all means, take them.) This is not a book that will suggest the solution to your overwhelm is better time management, a more positive attitude, or learning to lean in harder. You've probably tried all of that. We all have. And yet here we are, still crying in our showers.

This is also not a book that will fix everything. I'm a realist. I'm writing this while navigating my own chaos—still missing Wyoming, still working on that house, still aching for my girls across the ocean, still building something from the ground up while managing health challenges and everything else life keeps throwing at me. I'm not going to pretend I have it all figured out, because I don't. No one does.

What I *can* offer you is this: decades of professional experience in psychology and Hypnotism, working with women who carry impossible loads. Practical tools that actually work—including many that cost nothing and take mere moments. The reassurance that you are not alone, backed up by the stories of women far more famous and successful than either of us, who have stood exactly where you're standing. And perhaps most importantly, permission. Permission to feel what you're feeling. Permission to admit that too much is too much. Permission to put yourself somewhere on your own priority list—even if, like me, you're supposed to be the strong one.

This book is for the woman who is exhausted but keeps going. For the woman who answers "Fine" when people ask how she is, because explaining the truth would take too long, and she doesn't have the energy anyway. For the woman who lies awake at 3 a.m. with her mind racing through everything she hasn't done, everything she needs to do, everything that might go wrong if she drops any of the balls she's juggling. For the woman who has moved somewhere new and left her people behind. For the woman who spends her days helping others and has forgotten how to ask for help herself. For the woman who wonders if struggling at this stage of life means she's somehow failed.

This book is for you. Even if you're not sure you deserve it. *Especially* if you're not sure you deserve it.

SHE CRIED TOO

Serena Williams

"I am not OK today. And that's OK to not be OK. No one is OK every single day. If you are not OK today, I'm with you. There's always tomorrow."

Serena Williams—23-time Grand Slam champion, widely considered one of the greatest athletes of all time—posted these words to her 10 million followers. No preamble, no explanation, just raw honesty. She's spoken openly about postpartum depression, about crying when she couldn't find her daughter's bottle because she wanted to be perfect for her, and about still struggling sometimes. If the most decorated tennis player in history can say she's not OK, perhaps the rest of us can too.

I want to tell you something about the day I tested this book's title on a few friends. I didn't explain the concept. I didn't give any context. I simply asked, "Would you buy a book called *Crying in the Shower*?"

Every single one of them knew immediately what it would be about. No explanation needed. Their faces changed—that flicker of recognition of being *seen*. A few of them laughed, but it was the knowing laugh of women who understand. One of them just nodded slowly and said, "God, yes."

That's when I knew this book needed to exist. Not because I'm special or uniquely qualified (though I do have tools to offer you—we'll get to those). But because the experience is so universal, so shared, and so completely *hidden*. We're all doing this alone, thinking we're the only ones, when in reality we're part of a vast, silent sisterhood of women who are struggling and pretending we're not.

What would happen if we stopped pretending?

Before we go further, I want to address something. If you're reading this book, there's a chance—perhaps a significant one—that you're not just tired. You might be genuinely *unwell.* Overwhelm, left unchecked, can tip into something more serious: clinical depression, anxiety disorders, or burnout so severe it takes months or years to recover from.

This book will offer you many tools, and I believe they can help. But if you're experiencing persistent hopelessness, thoughts of harming yourself, an inability to function in daily life, or physical symptoms that won't resolve, please—and I say this with all the warmth in my heart—please also talk to a professional. Your GP. A counselor. A helpline. Someone.

Seeking help is not weakness. I'll say that again because I know you might not believe it: **Seeking help is not weakness**. Some of the strongest women I know are the ones who reached out when they needed support. Getting help is not admitting failure; it's choosing survival. It's choosing yourself.

Throughout this book, we'll explore when self-help is enough and when you might need something more. There's no shame in either path. There's only the path that's right for *you*, right now.

Here's what we're going to do together, you and I.

In the chapters ahead, we're going to look honestly at what you're carrying—not to make you feel worse, but because naming something is the first step to changing your relationship with it. We're going to explore why women in particular end up shouldering these invisible loads and why we're so convinced we should handle it all without complaint.

We're going to learn what's actually happening in your body and mind when you hit overwhelm—because understanding the physiology can help you recognize the warning signs earlier. We're going to examine the stories you tell yourself, the ones that keep you trapped in patterns of people-pleasing and perfectionism and putting everyone else first.

And then—this is the part I'm most excited about—we're going to fill your tool kit. Practical, usable strategies. Some take sixty seconds. Some cost nothing. Some you can do in the queue at the supermarket or sitting in your car before you walk into another meeting. Others are bigger shifts, for when you're ready for them. You'll get to choose what works for you.

By the end, I hope you'll still cry sometimes. (Crying is human. Crying is healthy. I'm not trying to turn you into a robot.) But I hope the crying will feel different. Less desperate. Less alone. More like a release than a collapse.

Most of all, I hope you'll know—really know, in your bones—that the shower doesn't have to be the only place you can be yourself. That struggle doesn't mean failure. That you deserve to be on your own list of people you take care of.

A few days after my shower breakdown, I mentioned the book idea to my daughter—one of those video calls that never quite bridge the distance but that I treasure anyway. I told her the title and watched her face on the screen.

She was quiet for a moment. Then she said, "Mum, every woman I know needs that book."

So here it is. For her. For my friends who nodded knowingly. For the women I've worked with over the years who taught me what resilience really looks like. For the strangers I'll never meet who are standing in their showers right now, crying, wondering what's wrong with them.

Nothing is wrong with you.

You're just carrying too much. And it's time we talked about it.

Throughout this book you'll find exercises and gentle invitations to reflect. I've gathered every single one into a free companion workbook — Wrapping Up Warm: A Companion Workbook to Crying in the Shower — yours to download at www.bighornwellness.com. Consider it my gift to you for showing up.

Turn the page when you're ready. I'll be right here.

Chapter Two

The Weight You're Carrying

If I asked you right now to list everything you're responsible for, you'd probably start with the obvious things. Your job, perhaps. The children, if you have them. The house. Maybe caring for a parent or a partner. The bills that need paying, the appointments that need making, the meals that need to appear on the table with suspicious regularity.

You could probably rattle off a decent list without much thought. These are the visible tasks—the ones that show up on to-do lists, the ones other people can see you doing, the ones that have a beginning and (theoretically) an end.

But here's what I've learned, both professionally and personally: the visible tasks are only the tip of the iceberg. Underneath the surface, invisible to everyone, including sometimes ourselves, lies a vast, cold mass of *everything else*. The mental load. The emotional labor. The anticipatory planning. The constant, low-level hum of responsibility that never quite switches off, even when you're supposedly relaxing.

This chapter is about making the invisible visible. Because you can't put down a weight you don't know you're carrying. And my guess is, you're carrying far more than you realize.

The Visible Load

Let's start with what's on the surface. The visible load is what most people think of when they imagine "being busy." It's the tangible stuff—the tasks you could, in theory, write on a list and tick off.

For many women, this includes some combination of paid work (whether that's a job, a career, a business, or the gig economy patchwork that keeps food on the table). Childcare—not just the being-with-children part, but the school runs, the homework supervision, the activity shuttling, and the endless laundry that seems to reproduce overnight. Housework—the cooking, cleaning, shopping, and maintenance that a home requires simply to function. And, increasingly, eldercare—supporting aging parents who need more help than they used to, coordinating their appointments, managing their medications, and being on call for emergencies.

If you're a sandwich generation woman—pressed between children who still need you and parents who are starting to—you might be doing all this simultaneously. If you're caring for a partner with health issues, add that to the pile. If you're building a business or pursuing a demanding career, layer that on top.

The visible load alone would be enough to exhaust anyone. But it's not the whole picture. It's not even close.

SHE CRIED TOO

Emily Nagoski

"The problem is not that women don't try. On the contrary, we're trying all the time to do, and be all the things everyone demands from us."

Emily Nagoski is a health educator and author of *Burnout: The Secret to Unlocking the Stress Cycle*, which she co-wrote with her sister Amelia. Their research focuses specifically on how women experience and carry stress differently. The book emerged from Emily's own burnout while working in academia—proof that even those who study overwhelm professionally aren't immune to drowning in it.

The Mental Load

Now we dive beneath the surface. The mental load, sometimes called "cognitive labor," is the endless invisible spreadsheet running in the background of your brain that no one else can see and no one gives you credit for.

It's remembering that your daughter's PE kit needs washing for tomorrow. It's knowing that the car is due for its annual Department of Transport check next month, and you should probably book that soon. It's tracking that you're running low on pasta and toilet paper and that one specific yogurt your partner likes. It's holding the family calendar in your head—who needs to be where, when, and with what equipment. It's remembering birthdays and not just remembering them, but actually organizing cards and gifts and sometimes entire parties.

It's the never-ending scroll of *things to remember* that starts when you wake up and doesn't stop when you go to bed—if anything, it intensifies at 3 a.m. when your brain decides that's the perfect time to remind you about the permission slip you forgot to sign.

Here's the thing about mental load: It's work. Real work. It takes cognitive resources. It occupies bandwidth that could be used for other things like, I don't know, having a thought that isn't related to someone else's needs. But because it's invisible, it's unpaid, unacknowledged, and often not even recognized as labor at all.

When your partner says, "Just tell me what needs doing, and I'll do it," that sounds helpful. And maybe it is, a bit. But notice what's still sitting with you—the task of *knowing* what needs doing. The tracking, the noticing, the remembering, the delegating. You've become the project manager of the entire household, and project management is a full-time job that you're doing unpaid, in addition to everything else.

I remember a client telling me, years ago, that she felt like she had a thousand browser tabs open in her mind at all times, and she couldn't close any of them. That image has stayed with me because it's so precise. The mental load isn't one heavy thing—it's a thousand small things, each one light enough to seem trivial, but together they consume your entire processing capacity.

• • •

The Emotional Labor

If the mental load is the invisible *thinking* work, emotional labor is the invisible *feeling* work. And in many ways, it's even more exhausting.

Emotional labor is managing other people's feelings. Smoothing over tensions at family gatherings. Being the one who notices when someone's upset and does something about it. Keeping the peace. Creating the atmosphere—making Christmas feel like Christmas, making birthdays feel special, turning a house into a home through a thousand small acts of care and attention.

It's remembering to ask your colleague about their sick mother. It's modulating your tone in emails so you don't come across as "too aggressive" (a note men rarely receive). It's smiling when you don't feel like smiling because someone needs you to be okay. It's absorbing your children's big feelings, your partner's stress, and your parents' anxiety, and somehow metabolizing all of it without passing it on.

It's being the *shock absorber* of the family. The one who takes the impact so others don't have to.

And—this is important—emotional labor often requires you to suppress your own emotions in order to manage everyone else's. You can't fall apart because someone needs you to hold it together. You can't express anger because it might upset the equilibrium. You can't admit you're struggling because then who would everyone else lean on?

So where do those unfelt feelings go? Where do your anger, your grief, your fear, and your frustration get stored when there's no space to express them?

Often, they go to the shower.

SHE CRIED TOO

Michelle Obama

"Women in particular need to keep an eye on their physical and mental health, because if we're scurrying to and from appointments and errands, we don't have a lot of time to take care of ourselves. We need to do a better job of putting ourselves higher on our own to-do list."

Michelle Obama served as First Lady of the United States for eight years while raising two daughters in the most scrutinized house in America. She's spoken openly about experiencing "low-grade depression," about the importance of therapy, and about the particular pressures women face to care for everyone except themselves. Even in the White House, surrounded by staff and support, she found herself scurrying from appointment to errand—and had to consciously choose to prioritize her own well-being.

The Anticipatory Labor

There's another layer still, one that gets talked about less but that many women will recognize immediately: anticipatory labor. This is the work of *thinking ahead*—not just managing what needs to happen now but constantly scanning for what might need to happen next.

It's the "what if" planning that runs on a loop in the background of your mind. What if the car breaks down—do we have breakdown cover? What if Mum falls—who would we call? What if the kids get sick during the school holidays—how would I manage work? What if, what if, what if.

Anticipatory labor is why you lie awake at night running through scenarios. It's why you always seem to be three steps ahead, seeing problems before they arise and quietly heading them off. It's why you pack snacks "just in case," keep acetaminophen and ibuprofen in your bag, along with the first aid kit, spare underwear, and know where the nearest toilet is in any building you enter.

This forward-scanning is protective—it keeps the household running smoothly and catches problems before they become crises. But it comes at a cost. Your brain never truly rests. You're always on alert, always preparing, always managing the future as well as the present.

I sometimes think of it as being an air traffic controller who never gets to clock off. The planes keep coming, and even when the skies look clear, you're watching for the next one.

The Weight of Worry

And then there's worry itself, which deserves its own mention because it's so often dismissed as "just" anxiety, as if the feelings weren't connected to anything real.

Women worry more than men. This isn't a stereotype; it's what the research consistently shows. We worry about our children, our parents, our partners, our jobs, our health, our homes, our finances, our relationships, and our futures. We worry about things we can control and things we absolutely cannot.

Some of this worry is socialized into us—we're taught from childhood that it's our job to care, to nurture, and to keep everyone safe. Some of it is structural. When you're the one holding all the information (the mental load), you're also the one who can see all the potential problems. And some of it is simply the rational response to carrying too much: when you have no margin for error, every potential disruption becomes a threat.

Worry is heavy. It sits on your chest. It steals your sleep. It accompanies you through your day like a low-grade headache you've almost stopped noticing. And yet it's rarely counted as "real" work. No one thanks you for lying awake worrying about whether you've saved enough for retirement or whether that mole on your child's arm has changed shape.

But worry takes energy. It depletes your reserves. It adds to the load you're carrying, even though it's entirely invisible to everyone else.

Why Women Carry More

Before we go further, let's address the elephant in the room: This isn't a universal human experience. It's disproportionately a *woman's* experience. Studies consistently show that even in households where both partners work full-time, women do significantly more housework, childcare, and emotional labor. The mental load falls disproportionately on women's shoulders. This isn't biology; it's culture—patterns passed down through generations, expectations absorbed before we were old enough to question them.

I'm not interested in blame here. Many of the men in our lives genuinely don't see the invisible work because they've never been taught to look for it. And many of us have been so thoroughly trained to carry it that we sometimes don't see it either—it just feels like "what women do."

But naming it matters. Understanding that this weight is real, that it's work, that it's disproportionate—this isn't about starting arguments. It's about giving you permission to take your exhaustion seriously. You're not tired because you're weak or because something's wrong with you. You're tired because you're doing three jobs while being credited for one.

The first step to changing something is seeing it clearly.

Making the Invisible Visible

So what do we do with all of this? The first step—and this might seem counterintuitive—is simply to *see* it. Not to fix it, not yet. Just to acknowledge the full weight of what you're carrying.

Most of us have never actually mapped out our load. We've never written down all the invisible tasks: the emotional labor, the mental tracking, and the anticipatory planning. It exists as a vague, overwhelming fog rather than a concrete list. And fog is impossible to tackle. You can't put down something you can't quite see.

I'd like to invite you to try something. Not right now, necessarily—but at some point when you have a quiet twenty minutes (I know, I know, you'll have to schedule it like an appointment). I want you to try mapping your load.

A GENTLE INVITATION

Mapping Your Load

This isn't homework. There's no grade, no right way to do it. But if you're curious about the true weight of what you're carrying, this exercise can be illuminating—and sometimes, surprisingly, a relief. Seeing it all on paper can make it feel more manageable than the fog in your head.

Find a quiet moment and four sheets of paper (or one sheet divided into quarters). Label them:

1. Visible Tasks — the tangible things you do that others can see

2. Mental Load — the remembering, tracking, planning, coordinating

3. Emotional Labor — the feeling-management, atmosphere-creation, peacekeeping

4. Worry & Anticipation — the what ifs, the forward-scanning, the contingency planning

Spend a few minutes on each, writing down everything you can think of. Don't censor yourself. Include the tiny things ("remembering to buy more bin bags") and the big things ("managing Mum's healthcare"). Include the daily tasks and the seasonal ones. Include the things you do and the things you think about.

When you're done, sit with what you've written. This is what you're carrying. All of it. Every day.

Some women find this exercise overwhelming. If that's you, please be gentle with yourself. You're not doing this to make yourself feel worse—you're doing it to understand why you're so tired.

Some women find it validating. Finally, proof that they're not making it up, that the weight is real. If that's you, let yourself feel that validation. You're not weak. You're carrying a lot.

I did this exercise myself a few months ago, during a particularly overwhelming stretch. I sat at my kitchen table with a cup of tea going cold and filled four pages with my microscopic handwriting. When I finished, I sat there for a long moment, just looking at it.

My first thought was, *No wonder I'm exhausted.*

My second thought was, *Why am I carrying all this alone?*

My third thought—the important one—was, *Something has to change.*

We'll talk about what that change might look like in later chapters. For now, I just want you to see what you're carrying. To understand that your exhaustion makes sense. That you're not failing at life—you're doing the work of three people and being given credit for half of one.

The weight is real. And you've been carrying it for a very long time.

I want to leave you with something before we move on. A thought that might feel uncomfortable at first, but that I hope will eventually feel freeing:

You are not required to carry all this.

I know. I know. The world has told you otherwise. Your upbringing has told you otherwise. The voice in your head that sounds suspiciously like your mother or your culture or every magazine you've ever read has told you otherwise. You're a woman, so you carry. That's just how it is.

But what if it isn't? What if some of this weight could be put down? Shared? Released? What if "good enough" could replace "perfect"? What if some balls are actually *supposed* to drop?

We're not there yet. There's more to understand first—about how we got here, about what's happening in our bodies when we hit overwhelm, and about the stories we tell ourselves that keep us trapped in these patterns.

But I wanted to plant that seed now: This weight you're carrying? Some of it was never yours to carry in the first place. And some of it you picked up so long ago you've forgotten you're even holding it.

In the chapters ahead, we'll start figuring out which is which.

Chapter Three

How Did We Get Here?

Here's a question I find myself asking, sometimes in the shower, sometimes at 3 a.m., sometimes while staring blankly at a to-do list that seems to have reproduced overnight: *How did it get like this?*

It's not a question of blame—or at least, it doesn't have to be. It's more a question of understanding. Because somewhere along the line, women ended up carrying the weight of the world on our shoulders while being told we should do it gracefully, gratefully, and with a nice manicure. And if we're going to change anything, it helps to understand how we got here.

This chapter is about tracing the threads—the historical, cultural, and personal forces that have conspired to put us in the shower, crying. Not to make you feel worse. Not to assign blame. But because seeing the pattern is the first step to stepping out of it.

The Roles We Inherited

Let's start with history because we didn't arrive here out of nowhere.

For most of human history, women's roles were constrained but at least somewhat defined. You knew what was expected: home, children, hearth. It was limiting, often oppressive, and I'm not for a moment suggesting we should go back to it. But there was a certain clarity. You knew what your job was, even if you had no choice in taking it.

Then something remarkable happened. Women fought for—and gradually won—access to education, careers, financial independence, and a political voice. Doors that had been locked for centuries slowly creaked open. Our grandmothers and great-grandmothers pushed and pushed until we could be doctors, lawyers, executives, politicians, and astronauts. We could have careers. We could have ambitions. We could have lives beyond the domestic sphere.

This was progress. This *is* progress. I'm genuinely grateful to stand on the shoulders of the women who fought those battles.

But here's what happened along the way: We added. We didn't subtract.

Women gained access to the world of paid work, but we didn't hand off the unpaid work at home. We gained careers, but we kept the housework. We got to have ambitions, but we were still expected to make the house feel like a home, remember everyone's birthdays, manage the emotional temperature of the family, and look after aging parents when the time came.

The new expectations were stacked on top of the old ones. And somehow, we were supposed to do it all.

The Superwoman Myth

Sometime in the late twentieth century, a pernicious myth took hold: the Superwoman. You might remember her from magazine covers and television shows—the woman who effortlessly balanced a high-powered career with perfectly behaved children, a spotless home, a satisfying marriage, and probably a side hobby like marathon running or gourmet cooking.

She was *having it all.* And we were all supposed to want what she had. More than that—we were supposed to *be* her.

The problem, of course, is that Superwoman doesn't exist. She never did. Behind every woman who appeared to have it all was either a small army of paid help, a family structure that was doing a lot of invisible supporting, or—most often—a woman who was quietly drowning while maintaining a polished exterior.

But the myth persisted. And it did terrible damage.

Because if Superwoman could do it all, and you couldn't, what did that say about you? If other women seemed to be managing—careers flourishing, children thriving, homes immaculate—and you were crying in the shower, clearly the problem was *you.* You weren't trying hard enough. You weren't organized enough. You weren't enough.

The myth turned structural impossibility into personal failure. It took a set of expectations that no human could actually meet and made each individual woman feel ashamed for not meeting them.

I bought into this myth for years. Maybe you did too. It's hard not to when it's everywhere—in the magazines, in the way we talk about successful women, and in the admiring way we describe someone as "I don't know how she does it." (Spoiler: She doesn't. Not really. Not without a cost that's being paid somewhere, by someone.)

SHE CRIED TOO

Jacinda Ardern

"I was overwhelmed by the fact that beyond New Zealand's shore, it triggered a discussion about how we make these decisions. I had particularly a few women say to me, 'Thank you for making it OK to say that I'm tired.'"

Jacinda Ardern became prime minister of New Zealand at 37, gave birth while in office, and led her country through its worst mass shooting and a global pandemic. In 2023, she resigned, saying she "no longer had enough in the tank." The world was stunned—not because a leader was exhausted, but because one actually admitted it. After she stepped down, she said she slept well "for the first time in a long time." Even at the highest levels of power, the expectation that women should keep going indefinitely eventually meets the reality that we cannot.

The Highlight Reel

If the Superwoman myth was damaging, social media has poured petrol on the fire.

I want to be careful here because social media isn't all bad. It connects us, informs us, and gives voice to people who might otherwise go unheard. I've found genuine community online; perhaps you have too.

But let's be honest about what we're looking at when we scroll. We're seeing highlight reels. Curated glimpses of the best moments, the tidiest corners, and the most photogenic meals. We're seeing people at their most put-together, not at 6 a.m. with unwashed hair and a child who won't stop crying.

And something in our brains—something ancient and unhelpful—compares. We compare our everyday to everyone else's best day. We compare our insides to other people's outsides. We see a woman posting about her promotion, her marathon, and her beautifully organized pantry, and we don't see the anxiety medication she takes, the marriage that's struggling, or the cleaner who comes twice a week.

We see the swan gliding serenely across the water. We don't see the frantic paddling underneath.

And so we conclude, once again, that everyone else is managing and we're the only ones falling apart.

The isolation of modern life makes this worse. In previous generations, women lived in a closer community. You saw your neighbors' real lives—the arguments, the unwashed dishes, the days when everyone was struggling. There was no pretending everyone else had it figured out because you could see that they didn't.

Now we live in our separate boxes, connected primarily through screens that show us fiction dressed up as reality. Is it any wonder we feel like we're failing?

The Messages We Absorbed

History and culture create the water we swim in. But each of us also carries personal messages—beliefs we absorbed so early they feel like facts, patterns we learned before we had words for them.

Think for a moment about what you learned about being a woman. What did your mother model? What did your father expect? What did your teachers praise you for? What did your family celebrate, and what did they criticize?

Many of us learned that good girls don't complain. That being helpful is how you earn love. That other people's needs come before your own. That keeping the peace is your job. That showing you're struggling is shameful. That your worth is tied to what you do, not who you are.

These messages weren't always spoken aloud. Sometimes they were absorbed through observation—watching our mothers martyr themselves, watching our fathers check out of domestic responsibility, and watching which behaviors got approval and which got criticism.

By the time we were adults, these beliefs felt like bedrock. Of *course,* you put others first. Of *course,* you don't ask for help. Of *course,* you keep going until you collapse. That's just... what you do.

But these aren't facts. They're patterns. And patterns can be changed, though first they have to be seen.

The Perfectionism Trap

One pattern deserves particular attention because it's so common among overwhelmed women: perfectionism.

Perfectionism sounds almost like a virtue, doesn't it? Having high standards. Wanting to do things well. Taking pride in your work. What's wrong with that?

Nothing, except that's not really what perfectionism is. True perfectionism isn't about healthy striving. It's about the belief that if you do everything perfectly, you can avoid criticism, failure, or pain. It's about trying to earn your worth through achievement. It's about the terror of being seen as anything less than competent, capable, and in control.

Perfectionism is a defense mechanism. And like most defense mechanisms, it comes at a cost.

If you're a perfectionist, you can't delegate—because no one will do it as well as you. You can't lower your standards—because then you might be criticized. You can't admit you're struggling—because that would be failure. You can't ask for help—because that would mean admitting you can't handle things on your own.

Perfectionism keeps you trapped in the pattern of carrying too much because putting anything down feels like failure. It raises the bar higher and higher so that no matter how much you achieve, it's never enough. It tells you that the answer to overwhelm is to try harder, do better, be more—when the real answer might be to let some things be good enough.

I recognize this pattern in myself. Perhaps you do too. It's exhausting to admit how much of my overwork has been driven not by necessity but by the fear of being seen as anything less than capable. How many tasks I've taken on not because they needed doing but because I couldn't bear the thought of someone thinking I couldn't handle them.

The People-Pleasing Pattern

Hand in hand with perfectionism often comes people-pleasing—the compulsive need to make others happy, often at the expense of your own well-being.

People-pleasers say yes when they mean no. They take on tasks they don't have the capacity for because they can't bear to disappoint. They prioritize everyone else's comfort over their own, then wonder why they're so depleted.

Like perfectionism, people-pleasing often has its roots in childhood. Maybe love felt conditional on being good, helpful, and easy. Maybe conflict was scary, and keeping everyone happy was how you stayed safe. Maybe you learned early that your needs mattered less than other people's, and you've been living that lesson ever since.

The tragedy of people-pleasing is that it doesn't even work. You bend yourself into a pretzel trying to make everyone happy, and someone's still disappointed. Often, that someone is you. But by then, you've given away so much of yourself that there's nothing left.

Every time you say yes when you mean no, you betray yourself a little. Every time you put someone else's needs ahead of your own—not from genuine generosity but from compulsion—you teach yourself that you don't matter. Is it any wonder that women who've spent decades doing this end up crying in showers?

When Life Compounds Everything

On top of all this—the historical weight, the cultural myths, the personal patterns—life sometimes throws in extra challenges. And these can take a load that was already too heavy and make it unbearable.

- Illness. Your own or someone you love.
- Caregiving. Children with additional needs, aging parents, and partners whose health is changing.
- Financial stress. The grinding worry of not quite having enough, the exhaustion of making do, the impossible choices.
- Relationship difficulties. The loneliness of a struggling marriage, the grief of divorce, the complexity of blended families.
- Moving to a new place and starting over.
- Losing people you love.
- Facing your own mortality.
- Watching your children struggle.
- Navigating a world that seems increasingly chaotic and frightening.

These aren't excuses. They're not signs of weakness. They're *life*—the heavy, complicated, sometimes brutal reality of being human. And when they land on top of an already-overloaded system, something has to give.

What often gives is the woman at the center. Because she's been trained to absorb, to cope, and to carry. Because everyone's counting on her. Because she doesn't know how to stop.

The Permission Problem

There's one more piece to this puzzle, and it might be the most important: permission.

Many of us are waiting for permission to put something down. Permission to rest. Permission to say no. Permission to not be everything to everyone. We're waiting for someone to tap us on the shoulder and say, "You've done enough. You can stop now."

But that permission rarely comes. The world is quite happy to keep taking from you as long as you keep giving. Your family will keep accepting your labor as long as you keep offering it. Your workplace will keep piling on you as long as you keep saying yes. No one is going to tell you to stop, because it's not in their interests for you to stop.

The permission has to come from you. And that's terrifying because it means taking responsibility. It means choosing yourself—something many of us have never been taught to do.

Later in this book, we'll talk about how to give yourself that permission, how to set boundaries, and how to let some things go. But for now, I just want you to notice: if you're waiting for permission to stop carrying so much, you might be waiting forever. The permission won't come from outside. It has to come from you.

Seeing the Pattern

So how did we get here? Through a perfect storm of forces: Historical shifts that added new expectations without removing old ones. Cultural myths that told us we should be able to do it all. Social comparisons that made us think everyone else was managing. Personal patterns—perfectionism, people-pleasing—

that kept us trapped. Life circumstances that piled weight upon weight. And a lack of permission to put any of it down.

None of this is your fault. Please hear that. The exhaustion you feel isn't a personal failing. It's the predictable result of a system that asks too much and gives too little support. You were set up to struggle.

But—and this is where hope enters—just because it isn't your fault doesn't mean you're powerless. You can't single-handedly change history or culture (though you can contribute to that change). But you can start to see your own patterns. You can question the beliefs you absorbed. You can begin, slowly, to give yourself permission to do things differently.

Understanding how we got here is the first step. It moves us from shame ("What's wrong with me?") to clarity ("Oh, I see why this is so hard"). And clarity creates the possibility of change.

I want to leave you with a thought that took me a long time to really understand:

You are not struggling because you're not good enough. You're struggling because you're trying to meet impossible standards with insufficient support in a culture that refuses to admit the standards are impossible.

The game was rigged from the start. And realizing that—really taking it in—can be surprisingly liberating. Because if the game is rigged, maybe you can stop trying so hard to win it. Maybe you can make up your own rules instead.

In the next chapter, we're going to look at what all this weight is doing to your body and mind—the physiology of overwhelm.

Because understanding what's happening inside you is another piece of the puzzle, another step toward change.

But before we go there, I want you to take a breath. Maybe put a hand on your heart. And acknowledge: You've been carrying an impossible load, shaped by forces larger than yourself, for a very long time.

That's not weakness. That's survival.

And you're still here.

You've done the bravest thing — you've looked honestly at where you are. Now it's time to understand what's actually happening inside you when you carry all of this. That's what Part Two is for.

PART TWO

The Water
Understanding What's Happening

Chapter Four

Your Body Knows Before You Do

Here's something that might make you feel a little bit better: Your body figured out you were in trouble long before you did.

All those symptoms you've been trying to ignore—the tension headaches, the jaw you realize you've been clenching, the sleep that won't come even though you're exhausted, the heart that races when you're just sitting at your desk—they're not signs that something is *wrong* with you. They're signs that your body has been sending you messages, and you've been too busy to read them.

Or perhaps you read them and dismissed them. *It's just stress. Everyone's tired. I'll rest when this project is finished. This is just what life feels like at this age.*

I know. I did the same thing.

The thing is, your nervous system doesn't understand deadlines or responsibilities or the fact that you can't possibly fall apart right now. It only understands threat and safety, danger and rest. And when it perceives that you've been under threat for too long—that there's been too much demand with too little recovery—it starts sending increasingly urgent signals.

The problem is, most of us have become remarkably good at ignoring those signals. We've had to be. Who has time to listen to their body when there's a to-do list that never ends?

The Orchestra in Your Body

I'm going to get a bit science-y here, but I promise to keep it accessible. Understanding what's actually happening in your body isn't just interesting, it's validating. Because when you realize that your symptoms have a biological explanation, you can finally stop blaming yourself for not coping better.

Your autonomic nervous system—the one that operates beneath your conscious awareness, running all the automatic functions like breathing, digestion, and heart rate—has two main branches. Think of them as an orchestra with two different conductors, each creating a completely different musical experience.

The first conductor is your **sympathetic nervous system**. This is your body's accelerator. It's the conductor who leads the urgent, driving pieces—the music that makes your heart pound and your muscles tense. When this conductor takes over, your body prepares for action: fight, flight, or freeze. Your heart beats faster. Your breathing becomes shallow. Blood flows to your large muscles, away from your digestive system (which is why stress kills your appetite or makes your stomach churn). Your pupils dilate. Your senses sharpen. Everything nonessential gets put on hold.

This is the music of emergency. It's supposed to play when a tiger is chasing you, then stop when you've escaped to safety.

The second conductor is your **parasympathetic nervous system**. This is your body's brake. It's the conductor who leads the gentle, restorative pieces—the music of rest, digestion, recovery, and repair. When this conductor takes over, your heart rate slows. Your breathing deepens. Your muscles relax. Your digestive system comes back online. Your immune system gets to work. This is the music of safety and recovery.

In an ideal world, these two conductors take turns appropriately. The sympathetic system ramps up for challenges, then hands the baton back to the parasympathetic system for recovery. Challenge and rest. Stress and recovery. Tension and release.

But here's what happens when you're chronically overwhelmed: the first conductor never puts down the baton.

The emergency music just keeps playing. And playing. And playing. Day after day, week after week, month after month. Your body stays in a state of high alert, waiting for a danger that never actually arrives (or never actually leaves), burning through resources that never get replenished.

And eventually, the orchestra starts to break down.

SHE CRIED TOO

Brené Brown

"In 2007, I had what I very dramatically call a 2007 breakdown. My therapist called it a spiritual awakening. I prefer breakdown. It came right after the TED talk. I was trying to outrun my own research."

Dr. Brené Brown—the world-renowned researcher on vulnerability and shame, whose TED talk on vulnerability is one of the most viewed in history—had spent years studying what makes people resilient. And then her body said, "Enough." She describes the experience as a full unraveling, one she tried to prevent by working harder, pushing through, and being more productive. Her body knew what her mind refused to accept. She went on to write about this experience openly, normalizing the reality that even the experts on human connection can find themselves disconnected from their own needs.

The Bucket Theory (But Not the One You Think)

You've probably heard the metaphor of stress as water in a bucket—fill it too high and it overflows. It's a useful image, but it misses something important.

The real problem isn't just how full the bucket is. It's that *the bucket itself gets damaged.*

When you're under chronic stress, your body isn't just accumulating strain. It's actually changing—at the cellular level, at the hormonal level, and at the neurological level. The bucket develops cracks. It starts to leak. It loses its capacity.

Let me explain what I mean.

When you encounter a stressor, your body releases cortisol—the primary stress hormone. In the short term, this is helpful. Cortisol increases available energy, sharpens focus, and helps you deal with the immediate challenge. When the stressor passes, cortisol levels should drop back to baseline.

But when the stressors don't stop—when you're juggling work deadlines, caregiving responsibilities, financial worries, a sick child, your own health concerns, and the never-ending domestic labor—cortisol levels stay elevated. They become the new normal.

This is when things start to go wrong.

Chronically elevated cortisol affects your sleep, making it harder to fall asleep and harder to stay asleep—even though you're exhausted. It affects your immune system, making you more susceptible to every bug that goes around. It affects your digestion, leading to everything from acid reflux to IBS symptoms. It affects your brain, impacting memory, concentration, and emotional regulation. It affects your metabolism, often leading to weight changes that have nothing to do with what you're eating.

And here's the cruelest irony: Chronic stress actually makes your stress response system less effective. You become simultaneously more reactive (jumping at small things) and less resilient (unable to recover quickly). The bucket gets smaller while the demands keep growing.

The Messages You've Been Missing

Your body has been talking to you. It may have started with whispers. If those were ignored, it moved on to clear statements. If those were ignored, it may have started shouting.

Here are some of the messages chronic stress and overwhelm send through the body. You might recognize a few:

Sleep disruption. Difficulty falling asleep because your mind won't stop racing. Waking at 3 a.m. with your heart pounding and thoughts swirling. Sleeping all night but waking exhausted. Any of these sound familiar?

Physical tension. Headaches that start at the base of your skull. Shoulders that have taken up permanent residence near your ears. A jaw you realize you've been clenching for hours. That spot between your shoulder blades that never unknots.

Digestive upset. A stomach that churns before difficult conversations. Appetite that disappears or becomes ravenous. IBS symptoms that flare during busy periods. The bloating and discomfort that seem to come from nowhere.

Immune system changes. Catching every cold that goes around. That virus you can't quite shake. The cold sore that reappears every time you're under pressure. Mysterious inflammations and flare-ups.

Heart and breathing. Heart racing when you're just sitting still. Shortness of breath when nothing physical is happening. That feeling of pressure in your chest that makes you wonder if you should be worried.

Cognitive changes. Walking into rooms and forgetting why. Struggling to find words you know perfectly well. Reading the same paragraph three times. Making silly mistakes you'd never normally make. That fog that makes everything feel slightly out of focus.

Emotional volatility. Crying at adverts. Snapping at people you love. Feeling numb when you should feel something. Anxiety that arrives without an obvious trigger. A sense of dread that doesn't lift.

I want to be clear: If you're experiencing any of these symptoms, please do get them checked by a doctor. They can have other causes that need attention. But if your doctor says, "It's just stress"—as if that's nothing—know that they're partly right and partly missing the point.

Stress isn't "just" anything. It's a physiological state that, when chronic, can affect every system in your body. Taking it seriously isn't weakness. It's wisdom.

I know this from personal experience. I was sitting at an appointment—one of many—with my husband, as his health has needed careful management, when he mentioned to our doctor that I'd seemed unusually tired lately and not quite myself. I was quietly furious with him. This was *his* appointment. I was fine.

Well. Our doctor—we share the same primary care provider—thought otherwise. She ordered a full set of blood tests for both of us.

I'm so glad she did.

It turned out my Vitamin D was very low, my B12 lower still, and my TSH was flagged too. Every single one of those results has a direct impact on energy levels, mood, and emotional resilience. I hadn't been imagining things. I hadn't been weak. My body had been running on fumes, and the blood work proved it.

All of these things, happily, can be simply addressed. But they had to be *found* first.

So here is my gentle but firm encouragement to you: Please do not save all your attention for everyone else's health. Not just *their* check-ups and their nutritional needs and their appointments. Yours too. *You* too.

No one can pour from an empty vessel—not even you.

SHE CRIED TOO

Selma Blair

"I was really struggling. I had pain. I was fatigued. I was depressed. I thought I was just a lazy, depressed person. For years, I told myself I wasn't trying hard enough."

Actor Selma Blair spent years pushing through symptoms she attributed to her own failings—exhaustion, pain, cognitive difficulties, and numbness in her limbs. She assumed she wasn't trying hard enough, wasn't strong enough, and wasn't disciplined enough. It took years to get a diagnosis of multiple sclerosis. While her situation is different from stress-related illness, her story illustrates something profound: Women are taught to dismiss their body's signals, to push through, to assume they're the problem. Our bodies know things our minds refuse to accept. Learning to listen is not indulgence—it's survival.

Why This Hits Women So Hard

Research consistently shows that women experience chronic stress and burnout at higher rates than men. This isn't because women are weaker, less resilient, or less capable of handling pressure. It's because the *pressures are different.*

Remember that mental and emotional load we talked about in Chapter Two? The invisible spreadsheet, the thousand open tabs, the project management of family life that no one thanks you for? Your nervous system doesn't distinguish between "real" stress and this kind of cognitive burden. It all registers as demand. It all requires resources.

Add to this the reality that women are often still the primary caregivers for children, for elderly parents, for partners, for the emotional well-being of everyone around them and the math becomes impossible. There simply aren't enough hours in the day, enough energy in the tank, enough of you to go around.

And yet we keep trying. We keep finding more to give. We keep saying yes.

Until our bodies say no.

Here's something I want you to sit with: when your body breaks down, it isn't failing you. It's *protecting* you. It's doing the only thing it can do when the demands exceed the capacity for so long that something has to give. It's forcing the rest you wouldn't give yourself.

I know that doesn't make it less frightening, or less inconvenient, or less frustrating. But maybe it can make it less shameful. Your body isn't betraying you. It's trying to save you.

Your Window of Tolerance

There's a concept in psychology called the "window of tolerance," and understanding it might help explain a lot about how you've been feeling.

Your window of tolerance is the zone in which you can function effectively. Within this window, you can think clearly, regulate your emotions, respond rather than react, and deal with life's ordinary stresses without falling apart. The window isn't about being calm all the time—you can experience stress, challenges, and even strong emotions within your window. You're just able to manage them.

Above the window is **hyperarousal**—the zone of anxiety, panic, overwhelm, racing thoughts, and anger that flares too quickly, that feeling of being wired and unable to calm down. This is the sympathetic nervous system in overdrive.

Below the window is **hypoarousal**—the zone of numbness, depression, disconnection, exhaustion, brain fog, that feeling of just... not caring anymore. This is what happens when your system gets so overwhelmed that it shuts down.

Here's the crucial thing: Chronic stress shrinks your window of tolerance.

Things that you used to handle easily now push you out of your window. You find yourself tipping into hyperarousal (anxiety, irritability, overwhelm) or hypoarousal (numbness, disconnection, shutdown) more easily, more often, over smaller triggers. Your capacity has genuinely decreased, not because you're weak but because your nervous system is exhausted.

If you've been wondering why you can't seem to handle things that you used to manage without a second thought, this is why.

Your window has shrunk. You're not imagining it. You're not being dramatic. You're living in a smaller space than you used to, and everything feels more cramped as a result.

The good news? Your window can expand again. With rest, with support, and with the strategies we'll explore in Part Three, you can rebuild your capacity. But that requires first acknowledging that your capacity has been depleted—and that depleting it further won't make things better.

When the Past Lives in the Body

There's something else that can shrink your window of tolerance—something that may have happened long before your current overwhelm began.

In his groundbreaking book *The Body Keeps the Score*, psychiatrist Bessel van der Kolk explores how trauma—and I'm using that word broadly—lives not just in our memories but in our bodies. Our nervous systems remember what our conscious minds may have forgotten, minimized, or never fully processed.

And here's what's important to understand: Trauma isn't just the dramatic events we typically associate with the word. It's not only war, or abuse, or catastrophic loss—though it certainly includes those things. Trauma can also be the accumulation of smaller wounds: a childhood where your emotions were dismissed, a relationship where you learned your needs didn't matter, and experiences of being unseen or unheard or unsafe in ways that were never acknowledged.

If you grew up in an environment where you had to be hypervigilant—always scanning for danger, always managing someone else's emotions, always trying to keep the peace—your nervous system may have been running in emergency mode for decades before adult life added its own demands. Your window of tolerance may have been narrower from the start, not because of any failing on your part, but because your system learned early that the world wasn't safe.

This might explain why you've always felt like you were working harder than everyone else just to stay level. Why other women seem to handle things that flatten you. Why you've carried a sense of *not quite coping* for as long as you can remember, even before life got objectively difficult.

If this resonates with you, I want you to know two things.

First: This is not something to push through alone. If past experiences are contributing to your current overwhelm, working with a trauma-informed therapist can be genuinely transformative. This isn't about dwelling in the past or assigning blame. It's about helping your nervous system finally learn that the danger has passed, that safety is possible, and that you don't have to keep running the old emergency programs.

Second: The strategies in this book can still help you, even if deeper work is also needed. Learning to regulate your nervous system, expanding your window of tolerance, and building in recovery are practices that support healing at every level. They're not a replacement for professional support if you need it, but they're not irrelevant either. Think of them as complementary: The daily practices that help you function while you do the deeper work or that help you maintain what you've healed.

Your body has been keeping score for a long time. That's not a character flaw—it's survival. And the fact that you're still here, still functioning, still caring for others despite carrying all of this? That's not evidence of weakness. That's evidence of extraordinary strength.

You just shouldn't have to do it alone anymore.

A GENTLE INVITATION

Listening to Your Body

Find a quiet moment, even five minutes. Sit or lie down comfortably. Take a few slow breaths.

Now, starting at the top of your head, slowly move your attention down through your body. Not trying to change anything. Just noticing.

Your forehead — is it tense or relaxed? Your jaw — clenched or soft? Your shoulders — up near your ears or dropped? Your chest — tight or open? Your stomach — churning or settled? Your hands — gripping or loose?

Whatever you find, you're not doing it wrong. You're just gathering information. Your body has been sending you messages. This is you learning to read them.

You might want to do this regularly—at the same time each day, perhaps. Not to judge but to learn. To notice patterns. To catch the whispers before they become shouts.

The Recovery Debt

There's one more concept I want to introduce because I think it explains something many women struggle with.

You've probably heard of sleep debt—the idea that when you don't get enough sleep, the deficit accumulates, and you can't just catch up with one good night. Recovery debt works the same way.

Every time you push through when you're tired, work through lunch, stay up late to finish something, give away your weekend to everyone else's needs, or skip the things that refill you, you're adding to your recovery debt. You're borrowing from your future capacity to meet today's demands.

And like any debt, it accumulates interest.

The longer you go without rest, the more rest you need. The more you deplete your reserves, the harder they are to rebuild. This is why "just getting through this week" becomes "just getting through this month" becomes "just getting through this year" becomes... this is just life now.

If you're feeling like you can't afford to rest—that there's too much to do, too many people depending on you, too much at stake—I understand. I've been there. I've said those exact words.

But here's what I've learned, the hard way: You can't afford *not* to rest. Because the interest on a recovery debt eventually becomes unpayable and the body forecloses. It doesn't ask permission. It just stops.

And a forced stop is so much harder than a chosen pause.

When I first learned about these concepts—the nervous system, the window of tolerance, recovery debt—something in me felt both relieved and furious.

Relieved because it explained so much. Why I couldn't sleep even though I was exhausted. Why I was snapping at people I loved. Why my body kept breaking down in inconvenient ways. Why I felt like I was losing my mind.

Furious because *no one had told me this before.* I'd been treating my symptoms as personal failures—as evidence that I wasn't coping well enough, wasn't strong enough, and wasn't managing like other women seemed to manage. When really, my body was doing exactly what bodies do when they've been running on empty for too long.

I wonder if you're feeling something similar right now.

Maybe recognition. Maybe validation. Maybe a creeping realization that things have been worse than you've been admitting, even to yourself.

If so, that's okay. In fact, it's more than okay—it's the beginning.

Because you can't address something you haven't acknowledged. You can't heal what you haven't named. And you've just done both.

In the next chapter, we'll look at the stories we tell ourselves—the internal narratives that keep us trapped in cycles of overwork and overwhelm. But before we go there, I want to leave you with this:

Your body is not your enemy. It is not betraying you. It is not weak, broken, or defective.

Your body is the only home you have in this world, and it has been trying to protect you the only way it knows how.

Maybe it's time to start listening.

Maybe it's time to stop treating rest as laziness, boundaries as selfishness, and breaking down as failure.

Maybe it's time to thank your body for carrying you this far and to ask it—gently, kindly—what it needs.

The answer might surprise you.

Or maybe it won't.

Maybe you've known all along.

Chapter Five

The Stories We Tell Ourselves

There's a voice in your head. You know the one.

It's the voice that says, *You should be able to handle this.* The one that whispers, *Other women manage just fine* when you're struggling. The one that hisses, *Who do you think you are?* when you dare to want something for yourself.

It sounds like a truth. It feels like a fact. It speaks with such authority that you rarely think to question it.

But here's the thing: That voice isn't telling you the truth. It's telling you a *story*—one you learned so long ago you've forgotten it was ever taught. A story that has shaped your choices, your limits, and your sense of what you deserve, without you ever consciously agreeing to believe it.

In this chapter, we're going to meet that voice. We're going to listen to what it says, trace where it came from, and—gently, carefully—begin to question whether it's been telling you the truth all along.

This isn't about silencing the voice. (Spoiler: That doesn't really work.) It's about changing your relationship with it. Learning to hear it without obeying it. Recognizing it as a story rather than a fact.

Because the stories we tell ourselves have enormous power. They can keep us trapped in cycles of overwhelm, or they can set us free.

The Greatest Hits

Let me introduce you to some of the most common stories overwhelmed women tell themselves. See if any sound familiar.

"I should be able to handle this."

This is perhaps the most universal story of all. No matter how much is on your plate, no matter how impossible the demands, there's a voice insisting that a better, stronger, more competent version of you would be managing just fine. The problem isn't the situation—it's you.

But let me ask you this: If a friend came to you carrying everything you're carrying, would you tell her she should be handling it better? Or would you be amazed she's still standing?

"Other women manage."

Ah, the comparison trap. You look around and see women who appear to have it together—the colleague who's always composed, the mother at school drop-off who looks like she's stepped out of a magazine, the friend whose social media shows a life of effortless abundance—and you conclude that the problem must be you.

But you're comparing your inside to their outside. You're comparing your unfiltered reality to their curated performance. You have no idea what's happening in their showers.

"I can't let anyone down."

This one keeps you saying yes when you mean no. It keeps you volunteering for things you don't have capacity for, staying late when you're exhausted, and putting everyone else's needs before your own until there's nothing left for yourself.

But here's a question worth sitting with: In your desperate effort not to let anyone down, who *are* you letting down? Because I suspect there's someone—and I suspect it's you.

"If I just try harder/work smarter/get more organized..."

The seductive promise of optimization. If you could just find the right system, the right app, and the right morning routine, surely you could fit it all in. The problem is efficiency, and the solution is trying harder.

But you can't optimize your way out of an impossible situation. You can't time-manage your way to having more hours in the day. Sometimes the answer isn't to try harder—it's to acknowledge that you're trying to do too much.

"I don't deserve rest until everything is done."

The cruel catch-22. You'll rest when you've earned it—when the to-do list is complete, when everyone's needs are met, when everything is taken care of. But the list is never complete. The needs are never fully met. And so rest becomes something you're perpetually almost qualified for, but never quite.

Meanwhile, you're running on fumes, wondering why you feel so depleted.

"Asking for help means I've failed."

Independence as identity. You've built your sense of self on being capable, competent, the one who copes. Needing help feels like an admission of defeat, evidence that you're not as strong as you should be.

But humans are not designed to function in isolation. We're wired for community, for interdependence, for sharing the load. Asking for help isn't failure—it's wisdom. It's what healthy people do.

SHE CRIED TOO

Glennon Doyle

"I was a human lie—living two lives. One was the life I let people see, and the other was the life I was actually living. I was dying of trying to appear okay."

Before she became the bestselling author of *Untamed* and founder of a movement, Glennon Doyle was drowning in secrets—addiction, bulimia, despair—while maintaining a perfect exterior. The story she told herself was that she had to hold it all together, that falling apart wasn't an option, and that asking for help would mean admitting she wasn't the person everyone believed her to be. Her breakdown became her breakthrough only when she stopped believing the story that she had to manage alone. She went on to build a life around the radical honesty she'd once been terrified to practice.

Where These Stories Come From

These stories feel like fundamental truths about who you are and how the world works. But they're not truths—they're learned beliefs. And anything that was learned can, with patience, be unlearned.

Some of these stories came from your family of origin. Perhaps you grew up in a household where emotions were dismissed, where needing help was seen as weakness, and where your worth was tied to your achievements or your usefulness. Children are remarkably good at absorbing the unspoken rules of their environment, and those rules can become the invisible architecture of adult life.

In psychology, we sometimes call these absorbed beliefs *introjections*—messages from significant figures in our past that we've swallowed whole, without chewing, without questioning. They sit inside us and speak with voices that sound like our own but aren't really.

I'll give you an example from my own life.

Every time I stand up to teach at a conference, or when I'm training other Hypnotists, or doing a demonstration somewhere, a thought sneaks into my mind. *Who are you to teach these people? Who do you think you are that these people can learn anything from you?*

I know what this is. I know *who* it is. It's my father's voice, absorbed decades ago, still playing on loop in moments when I dare to step into my expertise. It's an introjection—not a truth about my capabilities, but an old recording that never got updated.

And here's the important thing: Knowing what it is doesn't make it disappear. The voice still comes. The difference is that now I know how to meet it. I can hear it without obeying it. I can acknowledge its presence without letting it run the show.

That's what I want for you, too.

Some stories came from a broader culture. The superwoman myth we discussed earlier. The messages about what good women do, how good mothers behave, and what successful people look like. We've absorbed a lifetime of images and expectations, many of them contradictory, most of them impossible, and all of them presented as if they were simply the way things are.

And some stories came from painful experiences. If you were once let down badly when you asked for help, you may have concluded that asking for help is dangerous. If you were once criticized harshly for a mistake, you may have decided that mistakes are unacceptable. We build protective stories from our wounds—and then we forget they were ever a choice.

The Voice That Isn't Yours

Here's something worth considering: that critical voice in your head, the one that tells you you're not good enough, not coping well enough, not trying hard enough—whose voice is it really?

If you listen closely, you might recognize it. It might sound like a parent, a teacher, an ex-partner, a childhood bully. It might be an amalgamation of all the people who ever made you feel small. It might be the voice of a culture that profits from your self-doubt.

The point isn't to assign blame. The point is to recognize that this voice isn't *you.* It's a tenant who moved in so long ago you forgot they weren't family. It's a program running in the background, written by someone else, that you never consciously installed.

You don't have to evict it entirely. (Good luck with that—these voices are remarkably persistent.) But you can start to notice it as separate from yourself. You can hear it say. *Who do you think you are?* and respond, internally, *Ah, there you are again. Thanks for your input. I'm going to do this anyway.*

This is the beginning of freedom. Not the absence of the voice, but a new relationship with it.

SHE CRIED TOO

Viola Davis

"I spent most of my life feeling like an imposter. Even after the Emmy. Even after the Oscar. There was always a voice saying I wasn't really talented, that everyone was going to find out."

Viola Davis—one of the most acclaimed actors of her generation and the first Black woman to win an Emmy, Oscar, and Tony Award—has spoken openly about battling imposter syndrome throughout her career. Despite extraordinary external validation, the internal voice persisted: *Not good enough, not really talented, about to be exposed.* Her story illustrates something profound: The voice that tells us we're not enough has nothing to do with whether we're actually enough. It's a story, not a fact. And even the most successful among us can be haunted by it.

The Cost of These Stories

These stories aren't just uncomfortable background noise. They have real consequences.

When you believe you should be able to handle everything, you don't ask for help until you're in crisis. When you believe other women manage better, you isolate yourself in shame rather than reaching out for connection. When you believe you can't let anyone down, you let yourself down, over and over, until there's nothing left.

These stories keep you overworking, over-giving, and over-functioning. They keep you running on empty and call it normal. They keep you believing that the solution to exhaustion is to try harder, when in fact the solution might be to try *less*—to do less, to expect less of yourself, and to allow yourself to be human.

The stories we tell ourselves shape the lives we live. And if the stories are unkind, the lives become unbearable.

Beginning to Question

So how do we start to loosen the grip of these stories?

First, we notice them. This sounds simple, but it's revolutionary. Most of the time, these thoughts happen so fast and feel so true that we don't even register them as thoughts. They're just... reality. The way things are.

Start paying attention to what you tell yourself when you're struggling. What's the running commentary? What are the judgments? If you wrote down the things you say to yourself, would you be horrified to see them in black and white?

Second, we get curious about the source. When that critical voice speaks, ask yourself: whose voice is this, really? Where did I first learn this? Is this something I actually believe, or something I absorbed before I was old enough to question it?

Third, we ask whether it's true. Really true. Not whether it *feels* true—feelings and facts are different things—but whether there's actual evidence for this belief. Would it hold up in court? Would you convict yourself based on this evidence?

And fourth, we ask whether it's helpful. Even if the story contains a grain of truth, is believing it making your life better? Is it helping you cope or keeping you trapped?

A story can be partially true and still be worth releasing. *I could be more organized* might be technically accurate, but if the story becomes *I'm a disorganized mess and that's why I'm struggling*, it's no longer helping you—it's just adding shame to an already heavy load.

A GENTLE INVITATION

Meeting Your Inner Critic

Over the next few days, try to catch yourself in moments of self-criticism. When you notice that harsh internal voice, pause and ask yourself:

What is it actually saying? (Try to capture the exact words.)

Whose voice does it sound like?

How old do you feel when you hear it?

Would you say this to a friend in the same situation?

You don't need to do anything with what you notice. Just notice. Awareness is the first step. You can't change what you can't see.

Rewriting the Story

Once you can see a story as a story—rather than as truth—you have a choice you didn't have before. You can choose to tell a different one.

This isn't about positive thinking or pretending everything is fine. It's not about replacing *I'm failing* with *I'm amazing!* when you don't believe it. False positivity is just another kind of lie, and your psyche knows the difference.

Instead, it's about finding a story that's both true *and* kind. A story that acknowledges the difficulty without adding unnecessary cruelty.

For example:

"I should be able to handle this" might become *"I'm carrying a lot right now, and it makes sense that I'm struggling."*

"Other women manage better" might become *"I don't actually know what's happening behind other women's closed doors."*

"I can't let anyone down" might become *"I matter too. My needs are allowed to exist."*

"Who do you think you are?" might become *"I'm someone who has worked hard, learned a lot, and has something valuable to offer—even if an old voice disagrees."*

These rewritten stories won't feel natural at first. They might feel forced, awkward, or even fake. That's okay. You've been telling yourself the old stories for decades—the new ones need time to take root.

Keep telling them anyway. Talk back to the voice. Offer yourself the compassion you'd offer a friend. Over time, the new stories will start to feel less foreign. They may never fully replace the old ones—but they can run alongside them, offering an alternative, a choice.

A GENTLE INVITATION

Rewriting One Story

Choose one critical story you tell yourself regularly—one that causes you particular pain or keeps you stuck.

Write it down exactly as it sounds in your head. Don't soften it.

Now, imagine a wise, loving friend who knows everything about your situation. What might they say instead? Write their version—something that's still honest but kind. Something that acknowledges difficulty without adding cruelty.

Keep this rewritten story somewhere you'll see it. When the old voice speaks, let the new one answer.

A Note on Persistence

I want to be honest with you: these voices may never fully go away.

I've been doing this work—personally and professionally—for many years. I still hear my father's voice when I stand up to teach. The difference is that now it doesn't stop me. It doesn't run the show. It's background noise, not the main event.

That might not sound like much. You might have been hoping for total silence, complete freedom, and a mind finally at peace.

But I want you to understand how significant this shift actually is. When the voice speaks, and you no longer automatically obey—when you can hear it, acknowledge it, even thank it for trying to protect you in its misguided way, and then do what you need to do anyway—that's freedom. Not the absence of the voice, but freedom from its control.

And here's the other thing: the more you practice this, the quieter the voice often becomes. Not silent, but quieter. It learns that you're not going to be bossed around anymore, and it starts to lose some of its power.

You've been listening to these stories for years, maybe decades. They won't change overnight. But they can change. That's the promise and the practice.

The stories we tell ourselves are powerful. They shape what we believe is possible, what we think we deserve, and how we treat ourselves when we're struggling.

But here's what I want you to take from this chapter: *You are not your stories.* You are the one who can hear the stories, question them, and choose whether to keep believing them.

That voice that says you're not enough? It's lying. It's been lying for a long time, and you've been believing it because you didn't know you had a choice.

Now you do.

You can't control whether the voice speaks. But you can control whether you let it have the last word.

In the next chapter, we'll look at what happens when the cup doesn't just overflow—but when it cracks. We'll talk about recognizing the signs that you've moved beyond ordinary overwhelm into something more serious and what to do about it.

But before we go there, I want to leave you with this:

You have been so much harder on yourself than you needed to be.

You have held yourself to standards you would never impose on someone you loved.

And maybe—just maybe—it's time to start speaking to yourself the way you speak to your dearest friend.

With kindness. With understanding. With the recognition that you're doing the best you can with what you have.

Because you are.

Chapter Six

When the Cup Doesn't Just Overflow—It Cracks

This is the chapter I debated whether to include.

Part of me worried it might frighten you—that naming the darker possibilities might make them feel more likely, more real, more inevitable. Part of me wondered if it belongs in a book that's meant to be hopeful and practical.

But then I thought about the women who need this chapter most. The ones who've been telling themselves they're fine, just tired, just going through a rough patch—while something inside them knows it's more than that. The ones who've been minimizing and pushing through and holding it together until they can't anymore.

Those women need someone to say, There's a line between struggling and breaking. And it's okay to admit you might have crossed it.

So this chapter is about recognizing when overwhelm has become something more serious. When the cup doesn't just overflow—it cracks. When you need more than self-help strategies and breathing exercises and well-meaning advice to rest more.

This chapter is about knowing when to ask for real help and understanding that doing so isn't failure. It's the bravest thing you can do.

The Difference Between Stressed and Broken

Everyone experiences stress. It's an unavoidable part of being human, and in manageable doses, it's not even harmful—it can motivate us, sharpen our focus, and help us rise to challenges.

But there's a point where stress tips into something else. Where the normal human experience of feeling pressured becomes a clinical state that affects your ability to function. Where coping strategies stop working because you've moved beyond the territory they were designed for.

The tricky thing is, this transition often happens gradually. There's rarely a dramatic moment where you think, *Ah, I've crossed the line.* Instead, you slowly adapt to feeling worse and worse, adjusting your baseline, telling yourself this is just how life feels now.

So how do you know when you've moved from stressed to something more serious?

Burnout: When the Pilot Light Goes Out

Burnout isn't just being very tired. It's a specific syndrome characterized by three main components, and recognizing them might help you understand what you're experiencing.

Exhaustion that rest doesn't fix. This isn't ordinary tiredness that a good night's sleep or a weekend off can address. It's a bone-deep depletion that persists no matter how much you rest. You wake up tired. You drag through the day. You go to bed exhausted. And the cycle repeats, day after day, with no relief.

Cynicism and detachment. You find yourself becoming increasingly negative, irritable, or emotionally distant. Things you used to care about don't seem to matter anymore. You might notice you're going through the motions at work, with your family, in your relationships—present in body but absent in spirit. There's a protective numbness, a sense of *What's the point?*

A sense of ineffectiveness. Despite working harder than ever, you feel like you're accomplishing less. Your confidence erodes. You doubt your competence, your decisions, your ability to do things you've done a thousand times before. The harder you try, the worse it seems to get.

If you're recognizing yourself in these descriptions, please know: Burnout is real. It's not a character flaw or a sign of weakness. It's what happens when a human being is subjected to chronic stress without adequate recovery for too long. It's predictable, it's common, and—this is important—it's recoverable.

But it usually doesn't recover on its own. It needs intervention: reduced demands, increased support, and often professional help to find your way back.

Demi Lovato

"It's okay to ask for help. I think that's something that people need to hear more often."

Singer and actor Demi Lovato has spoken openly about struggling with depression, addiction, and a near-fatal overdose while in the public eye. For years, she felt pressure to appear strong and successful, even when privately she was unraveling. Her recovery journey has included therapy, medical treatment, and long periods of rebuilding her life. Lovato often speaks about the moment she realized she could no longer pretend everything was fine. Her message is simple but powerful: Asking for help is not weakness—it's the beginning of healing.

Depression: When the Color Drains Away

Sometimes what looks like burnout is actually depression, or burnout has tipped into depression. The two can overlap and intertwine, but depression has its own particular signature.

Depression isn't just sadness, though sadness can be part of it. It's more like the color has drained out of life. Things that used to bring pleasure don't anymore. The future feels hopeless or empty. Everything requires enormous effort, even getting out of bed, even basic self-care.

You might notice:

Persistent low mood that doesn't lift, even when good things happen. A flatness, a greyness, a sense that you're watching your life from behind glass.

Loss of interest or pleasure in things you used to enjoy. Hobbies abandoned. Social connections that feel like too much effort. An inability to look forward to anything.

Changes in sleep—either sleeping far too much or struggling with insomnia. Changes in appetite—either eating for comfort or having no interest in food.

Difficulty concentrating, making decisions, or thinking clearly. A sense that your brain is wrapped in cotton wool.

Feelings of worthlessness or excessive guilt. A harsh internal voice that's become unbearable. A sense that you're a burden to others, that everyone would be better off without you.

And sometimes—and this is the part that's hardest to write and hardest to read—thoughts of death or suicide. Not necessarily active plans, but a sense that you'd rather not exist. That you'd like to disappear. That the pain of being alive has become too much.

If you're experiencing any of these things, please hear me: **This is not your fault, and help is available.** Depression is a medical condition, not a moral failing. It's treatable. You don't have to feel this way forever.

IF YOU NEED SUPPORT NOW

If you're having thoughts of suicide or self-harm, please reach out for support immediately:

In the US: National Suicide Prevention Lifeline: 988 (call or text)

In the UK: Samaritans: 116 123 (free, 24/7)

International: findahelpline.com for resources in your country

You can also go to your nearest emergency room or call emergency services.

You matter. Your life matters. Please reach out.

Anxiety: When Worry Becomes a Prison

Anxiety is a normal human emotion—that flutter of nerves before a big presentation, the worry when a loved one is late coming home. But for some women, anxiety becomes something more—a constant companion that never quiets, a background hum of dread that colors everything.

Generalized anxiety feels like your brain's alarm system is stuck in the "on" position. You worry about everything, often disproportionately to the actual threat. You catastrophize, imagining worst-case scenarios and then responding as if they're already happening. Your body stays tense, braced for danger that never quite arrives.

Panic attacks are more acute—sudden surges of intense fear with physical symptoms so severe they can feel like a heart attack. Racing heart, difficulty breathing, chest pain, dizziness, and a sense that you're dying or going crazy. They can come out of nowhere, and the fear of having another one can become its own prison.

If anxiety is significantly impacting your daily life—if it's affecting your ability to work, to parent, to maintain relationships, or to leave the house—that's a sign it's moved beyond normal worry into something that deserves professional attention.

SHE CRIED TOO

Lady Gaga

"I have PTSD. I have chronic pain. I have had to learn to cope with a mental illness that I probably should have been treating for a long time. I was not okay, and I was pretending to be okay."

Lady Gaga—one of the most successful artists of her generation—has been open about her struggles with PTSD following sexual assault, chronic pain from fibromyalgia, and severe depression that at times left her unable to function. At the height of her fame, she was secretly falling apart. She's spoken about the danger of the myth that successful people don't struggle and the importance of seeking help even when—especially when—you're supposed to have it all together. Her documentary showed her in moments of complete breakdown, deliberately challenging the idea that celebrities somehow transcend human vulnerability.

When Your Body Forces the Issue

Sometimes the breaking point isn't psychological—it's physical. Your body, having been ignored for too long, forces you to stop.

This might look like:

Chronic pain that has no clear medical explanation or pain conditions that flare dramatically under stress. Fibromyalgia, chronic fatigue syndrome, autoimmune flares, migraines that won't quit.

Repeated illnesses as your immune system, depleted by chronic stress, fails to protect you. You catch everything. You take longer to recover. You never feel quite well.

A health crisis that stops you in your tracks. A heart scare. A collapse. Something dramatic enough that you can't ignore it anymore.

I'm not saying all physical illness is caused by stress. That would be an oversimplification and, frankly, insulting to people with genuine medical conditions. But stress can trigger, exacerbate, and prolong physical problems. And sometimes, the body breaks down because that's the only way it can get you to stop.

If your body is sending you messages through pain, illness, or collapse, please listen. It's not betraying you. It's trying to save you.

Why We Resist Getting Help

If you've recognized yourself in any of the descriptions above, you might have noticed a familiar voice piping up:

It's not that bad. Other people have it worse. I don't want to take resources from people who really need them. I should be able to handle this on my own. What would people think?

These thoughts are so common they're almost universal. And they keep countless women from getting the help they desperately need.

Let me address them directly.

"It's not that bad." Says who? You've been normalizing dysfunction for so long that you've lost perspective on what 'bad' actually means. If you can't function the way you used to, if you're suffering, if you're barely holding on—that's bad enough.

"Other people have it worse." Other people's suffering doesn't invalidate yours. There's no finite amount of compassion in the world that you'd be stealing from more deserving recipients. Your pain matters, period.

"I don't want to take resources from people who really need them." You really need them. And here's the thing: getting help when your problems are smaller prevents them from becoming bigger problems that require more resources later. Early intervention is efficient intervention.

"I should be able to handle this on my own." Why? Humans are not designed to function in isolation. We're wired for connection, for support, for sharing burdens. The idea that you should be able to handle everything alone isn't a strength—it's a cultural myth that's hurting you.

"What would people think?" Some might think less of you; it's true. But those aren't your people. The ones who matter will think, *She was brave enough to ask for help. She took care of herself. She did what she needed to do.*

What Getting Help Actually Looks Like

If you've decided you need support, what does that actually mean? Here are some options:

Your GP or primary care doctor is often the first port of call. They can assess your symptoms, rule out physical causes, discuss medication if appropriate, and refer you to specialists. Don't minimize when you describe what's happening—be honest about how bad it really is.

A therapist or counsellor can help you process what you're experiencing, understand the patterns that contributed to it, and develop strategies for recovery. There are many different therapeutic approaches—CBT, psychodynamic therapy, EMDR, and somatic therapies—and finding the right fit might take some trial and error.

A psychiatrist specializes in mental health from a medical perspective and can prescribe medication if that's something you want to explore. Medication isn't right for everyone, but for some people it's genuinely life-changing—creating enough stability to do the other work of recovery.

Support groups, whether in person or online, can help you feel less alone. There's something powerful about being in a room (virtual or otherwise) with people who truly understand what you're going through.

Crisis services are there for acute emergencies. If you're in immediate danger, please use them. That's what they're for.

You might need one of these resources or several. You might need intensive support for a while, then lighter maintenance. Recovery isn't linear, and your needs will change over time. That's normal.

A GENTLE INVITATION

An Honest Assessment

Take a moment to honestly answer these questions. No one will see your answers but you.

How long have you been feeling this way? Weeks? Months? Longer?

Is it getting better, staying the same, or getting worse?

How is it affecting your ability to function—at work, at home, in relationships?

If your best friend described feeling exactly like you feel, what would you tell her to do?

Whatever your answers, you now have information. What you do with it is up to you—but please, take it seriously.

The Other Side Exists

If you're in the middle of burnout, depression, or a breakdown, it can feel like this is just how life is now. Like you'll never feel better. Like the person you used to be is gone forever.

I want you to know: the other side exists.

I've seen women come back from complete collapse. I've watched them rebuild, slowly and painfully, into lives that are actually *better* than they had before because the breaking forced them to let go of things that weren't working, to set boundaries they should have set years ago, and to finally prioritize their own well-being.

That's not to romanticize breakdown. It's brutal. I wouldn't wish it on anyone. But if you're in it, or approaching it, I want you to know that this isn't the end of your story. It's a crisis point that can become a turning point.

Recovery takes time. It's not linear. There will be setbacks. But it's possible.

And sometimes, falling apart is the only way to rebuild something stronger.

I've hesitated throughout this chapter, wondering how much to share.

But I think you deserve to know that I haven't just studied these things from a comfortable distance. I've lived some of them. I've had moments where the cup didn't just overflow—it shattered. When I had to admit that willpower and coping strategies weren't going to be enough. When I needed help.

Asking for that help was one of the hardest things I've ever done. It felt like admitting defeat, like proving all those critical voices right. But it wasn't a defeat. It was the beginning of something different.

I'm on the other side now—not because I'm special or stronger than anyone else, but because I finally stopped trying to do it alone. Because I accepted that being human means sometimes needing support. Because I learned that asking for help isn't a weakness—it's wisdom.

If you're struggling, really struggling, I hope you'll consider doing the same.

This chapter has been heavy. I know that.

But here's the good news: it's also the end of Part Two. We've spent three chapters in the depths—understanding the physiology of overwhelm, examining the stories that trap us, and recognizing when ordinary struggle becomes something more serious.

Now, in Part Three, we surface. We come up for air. We start building the tool kit that will help you not just survive, but recover and thrive.

Whether you're in crisis or just feeling the early warning signs, the strategies ahead are for you. They're practical, they're accessible, and they work—not as replacements for professional help when it's needed, but as companions to it, or as preventive measures that might help you avoid reaching breaking point in the first place.

You've done the hard work of looking honestly at where you are.

Now let's talk about where you can go from here.

Turn the page when you're ready. Part Three is waiting.

PART THREE

Coming Up for Air
Practical Tools and Strategies

Chapter Seven

The Micro-Moments

Here's what I'm not going to tell you: take a bubble bath, light a candle, practice self-care.

I mean, do those things if you want to. They're lovely. But if you're reading this book, you probably don't have time for a bubble bath. You're lucky if you get to shower without someone banging on the door. The idea of self-care as it's usually presented—spa days, meditation retreats, and long walks in nature—feels like a cruel joke when you're just trying to get through the day.

So this chapter is different. This is about the micro-moments—the tiny interventions that take seconds, not hours. The techniques that work *within* the chaos, not requiring escape from it. The things you can do in the school car park, in the toilet cubicle at work, or in the thirty seconds before you walk into a difficult meeting.

These aren't replacements for deeper work. They won't solve the underlying problems. But they can help you regulate your nervous system in the moment, shift your state when you're spiraling, and create tiny pockets of relief in otherwise overwhelming days.

The chapters in this section each address something specific. Chapter Seven is for the moments when you're right in the middle of it — overwhelmed, right now, today. Chapter Eight is for the mind that won't quiet down. Chapter Nine is for the exhaustion that comes from giving too much of yourself away. Chapter Ten is for the loneliness that no amount of busyness can fix. You don't have to read them in order. Go where you're needed most.

Think of them as emergency tools—the things you reach for when your wits are heading out the door on a tide of panic, and you need them back… right now.

Why Small Things Matter

When you're overwhelmed, the idea of adding anything else to your plate—even helpful things—can feel impossible. The thought of committing to a meditation practice or an exercise routine or regular therapy appointments might make you want to cry. *Where would I find the time?*

That's exactly why micro-moments matter. They ask almost nothing of you. They can happen in the gaps—the pause before you answer the phone, the moment between putting the car in park and opening the door, and the breath you take before responding to a difficult email.

And here's the thing: Small interventions, repeated consistently, add up. Each time you use one of these techniques, you're sending a signal to your nervous system that you're paying attention, that you're taking care of it, and that safety is possible. Over time, these small signals accumulate into real change.

You don't have to do all of these. You don't have to do any of them perfectly. Just find one or two that resonate, and start there.

Breath: Your Built-In Reset Button

Your breath is the one part of your autonomic nervous system you can consciously control. It's the bridge between the automatic processes running in the background and your conscious mind. Which means it's also a lever you can pull to shift your state.

When you're stressed, your breathing becomes shallow and fast—up in your chest, feeding the anxiety. When you deliberately slow and deepen your breath, you send a signal to your nervous system that the emergency is over, that it's safe to calm down.

This isn't just wishful thinking—it's physiology. Slow, deep breathing activates the parasympathetic nervous system (remember our orchestra conductor from Chapter Four?), triggering the relaxation response. Your heart rate slows. Your blood pressure drops. Your muscles begin to release.

TRY THIS

The Physiological Sigh

This is the fastest way to calm your nervous system in real time. It's what your body naturally does when you're crying and finally start to settle—that shuddering double inhale followed by a long exhale.

1. Inhale deeply through your nose.

2. At the top of that breath, take a second, shorter inhale to fully expand your lungs.

3. Exhale slowly and completely through your mouth.

One or two of these can shift your state in seconds. You can do it anywhere—no one will even notice.

TRY THIS

Box Breathing

Used by Navy SEALs and first responders to stay calm under pressure. Simple, portable, and effective.

1. Inhale for 4 counts

2. Hold for 4 counts

3. Exhale for 4 counts

4. Hold for 4 counts

Repeat for one to two minutes. If 4 counts feels too long, start with 3. The rhythm matters more than the duration.

Grounding: Coming Back to Now

When anxiety spikes, your mind often leaves the present moment. It races into the future, catastrophizing about what might happen. Or it drags you into the past, replaying old hurts and fears. Grounding techniques pull you back to the here and now—the only place where you can actually do anything.

TRY THIS

The 5-4-3-2-1 Technique

This uses your senses to anchor you in the present moment. Go through each sense, naming what you notice:

5 things you can SEE (the texture of the wall, the light through the window, your own hands)

4 things you can TOUCH (your feet on the floor, the fabric of your clothes, the cool metal of a door handle)

3 things you can HEAR (traffic outside, a clock ticking, your own breath)

2 things you can SMELL (coffee, fresh air, hand cream)

1 thing you can TASTE (toothpaste, tea, the inside of your own mouth)

By the time you've finished, your racing mind has usually settled. You're back in your body, back in the room, back in the present.

TRY THIS

The Cold Water Reset

Cold activates the dive reflex, which slows your heart rate and calms your nervous system. It's quick, effective, and requires nothing but a tap.

Run cold water over the insides of your wrists for thirty seconds. Or splash cold water on your face, especially your forehead and temples. Or hold something cold—ice cubes, a cold drink—in your hands.

It sounds too simple to work, but the physiological response is real. Your body can't maintain panic while simultaneously responding to the cold.

SHE CRIED TOO

Michelle Obama

"I have had to learn that my aspirations, my desires, my feelings matter just as much as everyone else's. For so long, I put myself last. I thought that was noble. But you can't pour from an empty cup."

Michelle Obama—former first lady, lawyer, author, and one of the most admired women in the world—has spoken openly about struggling with "low-grade depression" during the pandemic, about the importance of protecting small moments of self-care, and about learning that tending to her own needs isn't selfish. She maintains daily practices, including morning workouts (which she calls her "sanity"), time with close friends, and deliberate boundaries around her energy. She's been clear that these small, consistent practices aren't luxuries—they're what make everything else possible.

Your Memory Bank: The Instant State-Shifter

This technique is one of my favorites, and it's one I use constantly—in hospital waiting rooms, before difficult conversations, when supporting clients through their pain, whenever I need to shift my state quickly and reliably.

It works like this: Your brain doesn't fully distinguish between vividly imagined experiences and real ones. When you recall a happy memory in rich sensory detail, your body responds as if it's happening now. The same neurochemicals release dopamine, often oxytocin, creating a genuine shift in your internal state.

The key is to have your memories ready in advance. You don't want to be searching for a happy memory when you're already in crisis—you want to know exactly which three memories you can reach for instantly when you need them.

Here's how to find them: Think back through your life for moments of genuine joy, peace, love, or laughter. Not the moments you think *should* make the list—the wedding, the graduation—but the ones that actually light you up when you remember them. You'll know you've found the right memories because you'll find yourself smiling without trying.

One of mine is my youngest daughter giggling when she was about eighteen months old. I can see her face, hear the sound, and feel the warmth of her small body. When I bring that memory fully to life in my mind, something in my chest softens. The panic recedes. I remember what matters.

With practice, you can access these memories faster and faster. Eventually, just the thought of them—even a word or image associated with them—can trigger the shift. It becomes a shortcut to a different state.

A GENTLE INVITATION

Building Your Memory Bank

Find a quiet moment to identify your three go-to memories. For each one:

What do you see? (colors, faces, light, surroundings)

What do you hear? (voices, laughter, music, nature)

What do you feel in your body? (warmth, relaxation, someone's touch)

What's the emotion? (joy, peace, love, safety)

Practice recalling each one until you can drop into it quickly. These are now your emergency reserves—ready when you need them.

Movement: Even Tiny Amounts

Exercise is one of the most effective interventions for stress, anxiety, and depression. The research is overwhelming. But when you're in survival mode, the idea of going to the gym or following a workout routine can feel laughable.

So let's talk about micro-movement instead.

When stress hormones flood your system, they're preparing your body for action—fight-or-flight. Those hormones need somewhere to go. Even small amounts of movement can help discharge them, completing the stress cycle and signaling to your body that the threat has passed.

This might look like:

Shaking. Literally shaking your hands, your arms, your whole body. Animals do this instinctively after a threat—a dog shakes off fear, a gazelle trembles after escaping a predator. It looks silly. It works.

Walking. Even a two-minute walk changes your physiology. Around the block, to the end of the corridor and back, up and down the stairs once. Movement creates momentum.

Stretching. Reach your arms overhead. Roll your shoulders. Twist your spine. Your body holds tension in physical form; stretching helps release it.

Pushing against a wall. Stand facing a wall, place your palms flat against it, and push. Hard. Hold for several seconds. This engages the large muscles of your body and can help discharge the energy of anxiety or anger.

None of these requires gym clothes, time, or privacy. They're micro-doses of what longer exercise provides—and micro-doses are infinitely better than nothing.

Naming It to Tame It

Neuroscience research has shown that simply naming an emotion can reduce its intensity. When you say out loud or internally, "I'm feeling anxious," or "This is fear," or "I notice anger rising," you activate the prefrontal cortex, the thinking brain. This creates a small separation between you and the emotion, shifting you from being *in* the feeling to *observing* the feeling.

The language matters. "I *am* anxious" is different from "I'm *feeling* anxious" or "I *notice* anxiety." The latter creates distance. You're not the emotion; you're the one experiencing it.

When you're in a difficult moment, try narrating what's happening:

I notice my chest is tight. I'm feeling overwhelmed. My body is having a fear response. This is uncomfortable, but it will pass.

This isn't about suppressing the emotion or pretending it's not there. It's about creating enough space to respond rather than react. The feeling is still present, but you're no longer drowning in it.

SHE CRIED TOO

Emma Watson

"I'm serious about therapy. I can't recommend it enough. It's changed my life completely. I think everyone should have access to it."

Emma Watson has been open about using therapy and daily self-care practices to manage the pressures of growing up in the public eye. She's spoken about struggling with imposter syndrome, anxiety, and the relentless scrutiny of fame. Her approach isn't dramatic—it's consistent, small practices: therapy, reading, time alone, boundaries around work. She's been clear that taking care of her mental health isn't something she does when she has time; it's something she makes time for, because everything else depends on it.

Self-Hypnosis: Your Secret Superpower

I've saved this one for near the end because it's my professional specialty, and I don't want it to feel like a sales pitch. But I'd be doing you a disservice if I didn't include it, because self-hypnosis is one of the most powerful tools I know for managing overwhelming emotions and changing your state quickly.

Hypnosis isn't what you see on stage shows—no clucking like chickens, no loss of control. It's simply a state of focused attention and heightened suggestibility. You've been in hypnotic states many times without calling it that: absorbed in a book, lost in a daydream, driving on autopilot and arriving without remembering the journey.

Self-hypnosis allows you to deliberately access this state and use it to calm your nervous system, change unhelpful thought patterns, and resource yourself for difficult situations. Once you learn the basics, you can use it anywhere—eyes open, in public, in the middle of a stressful day.

I've included a detailed guide to self-hypnosis in the appendix of this book. I'd encourage you to explore it. It's a skill that takes some practice to develop, but once you have it, it's yours forever—a tool no one can take from you.

When I Use These Tools

I want to be honest with you: I use these techniques all the time. Not because my life is unusually stressful (though it sometimes is), but because I'm human, and being human means sometimes needing help regulating my nervous system.

I use them in hospital waiting rooms, sitting under fluorescent lights, waiting for test results, with my heart trying to climb out of my chest.

I use them before stepping into difficult client sessions—the ones where someone's pain resonates too deeply with my own, and I need to park my feelings so I can be fully present for them.

I used them recently when I accompanied a friend to hospital for tests and then chemotherapy. As I sat beside her, I felt my own fear rising—old fears, from when I had cancer at thirty-two and was given six months to live. (Thankfully, it was stage three, not four in the end. A great surgeon stopped the spread just in time.) Those fears don't serve me anymore. But occasionally, because I am human, they try to sneak back in.

In that hospital room, supporting my friend in her real battle was far more important than my old fears trying to hijack the moment. So I used the tools. I breathed. I grounded myself. I recalled a memory that shifted my state. And I was able to be there for her—present, calm, useful.

That's what these techniques offer: not the elimination of difficult feelings, but the ability to have them without being controlled by them. To acknowledge what's arising, choose how to respond, and show up as the person you want to be.

A GENTLE INVITATION

Choosing Your Tool Kit

From the techniques in this chapter, choose two or three that resonated most with you. These will be your starting tool kit.

Write them down somewhere you'll see them—a note on your phone, a card in your wallet, or a sticky note on your mirror.

Practice them when you're NOT in crisis. Like any skill, they work better when they're familiar. You don't want to be learning a technique in the middle of a panic attack; you want it to be automatic.

Then, next time you feel yourself starting to spin, reach for one of your tools. See what happens.

These micro-moments won't solve everything. They won't fix a life that's structurally impossible, or heal deep wounds, or change the external circumstances that are causing your stress.

But they can help you get through the next hour. The next meeting. The next difficult conversation. They can give you tiny pockets of relief in overwhelming days. They can start to teach your nervous system that you're paying attention, that you're taking care of it, and that regulation is possible.

And sometimes getting through the next hour is all we need to do.

In the next chapter, we'll go deeper—exploring self-hypnosis, visualization, and the cognitive techniques that can help you reclaim your mind from the chaos. But those are additional tools, not replacements for these.

These micro-moments are the foundation. Small things, done consistently, in the cracks of impossible days.

Start there.

Chapter Eight

Reclaiming the Mind

The techniques in the last chapter were about getting through moments—the quick interventions that can shift your state when you're spiraling. They're essential, and I hope you're already experimenting with them.

But there's deeper work available too. Techniques that don't just help you survive difficult moments but actually change your relationship with your own mind. That help you step back from the chaos of your thoughts, separate fear from reality, and connect with a version of yourself who has already made it through.

This chapter is where I share the tools that have been at the heart of my professional practice for years—and at the heart of my personal survival too. These are the techniques I reach for when the micro-moments aren't enough. When I need to go deeper.

Some of these practices take a bit more time and focus than the quick interventions. But they're worth the investment because they build something lasting. They teach your mind new patterns, create new neural pathways, and give you resources you can draw on for the rest of your life.

The Power You Already Have

Your mind is extraordinarily powerful—though not always in ways that serve you. The same capacity for imagination that can spin worst-case scenarios in the middle of the night can also create profound states of calm. The same ability to replay painful memories can be redirected to access resourceful, joyful ones. The same focus that gets hijacked by worry can be trained to anchor you in the present moment.

You already have everything you need. You just need to learn how to use it.

What follows are techniques for reclaiming your mind from the chaos—for becoming the director of your inner experience rather than its helpless audience. None of them requires special equipment, much time, or any particular talent. They just require practice and patience.

Self-Hypnosis: Demystified

I'm a clinical Hypnotist. It's been my profession for many years, and I've seen the extraordinary changes it can create. But I'm also aware that the word "hypnosis" carries baggage—images of swinging pocket watches and stage shows where people cluck like chickens, concerns about mind control, and losing yourself.

So let me tell you what hypnosis actually is. It's a natural state of focused attention and heightened receptivity. That's it. Nothing mystical, nothing dangerous, nothing that takes away your control.

You've been in hypnotic states countless times. When you're so absorbed in a film that you forget you're sitting in a cinema. When you're reading a book and don't hear someone calling your name. When you drive a familiar route and arrive without remembering the journey. These are all naturally occurring trance states—your attention narrowed, your critical faculty relaxed, your subconscious mind more accessible.

Self-hypnosis simply means learning to create this state deliberately and to use it for your own benefit. When you're in this receptive state, suggestions for calm, confidence, clarity, and resilience can bypass the busy, critical conscious mind and land more deeply. Changes that feel impossible through willpower alone become strangely achievable.

I've included a full guide to self-hypnosis in the appendix of this book—a step-by-step process you can learn and use for yourself. Here, I want to focus on what it can help with and why it's worth exploring.

Self-hypnosis can help you:

- Calm an overwhelmed nervous system more quickly and deeply than conscious relaxation techniques alone.
- Access resourceful states—confidence, calm, clarity—when you need them most.
- Change patterns of thinking that have been resistant to conscious effort.
- Prepare for challenging situations by mentally rehearsing them going well.
- Process and release difficult emotions that have been stuck.
- Connect with a deeper wisdom than the anxious, chattering surface mind.

Once you learn the basics—and they're not complicated—you have a tool for life. Something that's always available, requires no equipment, and can't be taken from you. I use it constantly, and I've seen it transform the lives of countless clients. It's one of the greatest gifts I can offer you through this book.

SHE CRIED TOO

Ruby Wax

"I've had three major breakdowns, been hospitalized, and wanted to die. But I've also learned that the mind can be trained. We're not victims of our brains—we can change them."

Ruby Wax—comedian, writer, and mental health advocate—has been in hospital for severe depression multiple times. After her third breakdown, she went back to university at Oxford to study mindfulness-based cognitive therapy, determined to understand her own mind. She emerged with a master's degree and a mission to destigmatize mental illness. Her message is that our minds are trainable—that the same brain that creates suffering can learn to create peace. She's living proof that even people who've been to the darkest places can learn to work with their minds rather than being controlled by them.

Visualization: Seeing Your Way Through

Visualization is the deliberate use of your imagination to create change. It works because, as I mentioned in the last chapter, your brain doesn't fully distinguish between vividly imagined experiences and real ones. The same neural pathways fire. The same neurochemicals release.

This is why worrying is so physiologically expensive—when you imagine disaster, your body responds as if it's happening. But it's also why positive visualization is so powerful—when you vividly imagine yourself calm, capable, and successful, your body begins to believe it.

Athletes have used visualization for decades. A skier mentally rehearses the perfect run. A tennis player imagines the serve landing exactly where intended. Research consistently shows that mental rehearsal improves actual performance, not as much as physical practice, but remarkably close.

You can use the same principle for the challenges you're facing.

Future Focus: Meeting the Woman Who Made It Through

This is one of my favorite techniques, and one I return to again and again—both in my own life and with clients.

The premise is simple. Somewhere in your future, there's a version of you who has already navigated the challenge you're currently facing. She's on the other side. She made it through. And she has wisdom to offer.

When we're in the middle of difficulty, it can be impossible to believe that things will ever be different. The fear and overwhelm are so loud that they drown out any other possibility. But your future self knows something you don't yet; she knows how the story unfolds. She knows you survive this. She knows what helped.

This visualization allows you to borrow her perspective. To see through her eyes for a moment. To feel what it feels like to have already made it through.

TRY THIS

Meeting Your Future Self

Find a quiet place where you won't be disturbed. Close your eyes. Take several slow, deep breaths until you feel yourself settling.

Now, imagine moving forward in time. Past this current difficulty. Past the struggle. To a point where you've navigated through and emerged on the other side.

See your future self clearly. Where is she? What does she look like? Notice her posture, her expression. She's been through what you're going through, and she's okay. More than okay—she's stronger for it.

Approach her. Ask her, *What do I need to know? What helped you get through? What can you tell me?*

Listen for her answer. It might come as words, as a feeling, or as an image. Trust whatever arises.

Before you leave, let her remind you: *You will make it through this. I'm the proof.*

When you're ready, slowly return to the present, carrying her wisdom with you.

This technique is powerful because it shifts your perspective from being trapped in the problem to observing it from a place of resolution. It reminds you that this current chapter is not the whole story. And it often brings to the surface wisdom that your conscious, worried mind couldn't access.

The Container: Parking What You Can't Process Yet

Sometimes we need to feel our feelings. And sometimes we need to park them temporarily so we can function.

This isn't the same as suppression or denial. It's a conscious choice to contain something for now, with the intention of returning to it later. It's what allows a surgeon to operate without being overwhelmed by the stakes. What lets a parent stay calm during an emergency. What enables you to get through a work presentation when your personal life is falling apart.

The container technique gives your mind a way to do this deliberately.

TRY THIS

Creating Your Container

Close your eyes and imagine a container. It can be anything: a treasure chest, a safe, a box with a heavy lid, a room with a strong door. Make it solid and secure—something that can hold difficult things without leaking.

Now, take the feeling, thought, or worry that's overwhelming you. Give it a form—maybe a color, a shape, a texture. And place it deliberately into your container.

Close the lid. Lock it. Know that it's secure.

Tell yourself, "This is safe here. I don't have to carry it right now. I can come back to it later, when I'm ready, when I have support, when the time is right."

You haven't made it disappear. You've just put it somewhere safe while you do what you need to do.

Separating Fear from Reality

Fear lies. Not always, but often. It takes a small possibility and inflates it into a certainty. It projects past pain onto future situations. It whispers *This will be terrible* about things that turn out to be fine, and *You can't handle this* about things you absolutely can.

The problem is, fear feels true. When your body is flooded with stress hormones and your heart is racing and your mind is spinning disaster scenarios, it's very hard to step back and evaluate whether the threat is real.

But this is exactly what we need to learn to do: Separate the fear, which is a feeling, a physical and emotional response, from reality, which may or may not match what the fear is telling us.

Here are some questions that can help create that separation:

What am I actually afraid of? Name the specific fear. Often our anxiety is a vague cloud of dread; pinning it down to specifics makes it more manageable.

Is this happening now, or am I imagining a future scenario? Most of our suffering comes from projecting into a future that hasn't happened yet. Right now, in this actual moment, are you okay?

What's the evidence for and against this fear? Not how it feels, but what's actually true. What facts support the fear? What facts contradict it?

What's the worst that could realistically happen? Could I survive it? Often, when we actually face the worst case, we realize we could cope. It would be hard, but we'd get through. The fear of the thing is worse than the thing itself.

Am I catastrophizing? Catastrophizing means jumping to the worst possible outcome without considering the more likely alternatives. Is there a more probable scenario that's less terrifying?

What would I tell a friend who was feeling this way? We're often much wiser and more compassionate with others than with ourselves. Access that wisdom for yourself.

These questions won't make fear disappear. But they can create a small space between you and the fear—enough space to see it as a reaction rather than reality. And in that space, you have choice.

SHE CRIED TOO

Oprah Winfrey

"I was completely burned out. I was running on empty. I had to learn to put myself on my own priority list. That was revolutionary for me."

Oprah Winfrey—arguably the most influential woman in American media—has been open about periods of complete overwhelm and the inner work required to manage them. She meditates daily, practices gratitude, and has spoken extensively about the power of visualization and intention-setting. She credits much of her success to learning to manage her mind rather than being managed by it. Despite her extraordinary external achievements, she maintains that the inner work is what makes everything else possible—and that learning to calm and direct her mind was one of the most important skills she ever developed.

When I Needed Every Tool I Had

I want to tell you about a time when I needed every single technique in this book—and some I probably invented on the spot.

In early 2019, I had my green card immigration interview scheduled at the American Embassy in Madrid, Spain. I'd been told I needed to apply from outside the USA, so my husband, Mike, and I had traveled there, along with our small white schnauzer, Alfred. We were staying in a tiny apartment in the old town, navigating an unfamiliar city, waiting for the interview I'd been anticipating for two years.

The day before the interview, Mike tripped over Alfred in Retiro Park. He cracked his head open and broke his collarbone. Mike had already had a stroke in 2017, so any head injury was terrifying. And the taxis were on strike. We had no car. No easy way to get anywhere.

Somehow, I got him to the hospital. While we were there, he had a seizure.

The hospital was overcrowded. No one spoke English. Mike needed to stay overnight. My interview at the embassy was at 8 a.m. the following morning—two miles from our apartment.

That evening, I walked the long journey back to the apartment alone. I left Alfred with water and food, gathered Mike's CPAP machine, and walked back to the hospital. Then I walked back to the apartment again, in the dark, in a city I barely knew. I don't know how many miles I covered that night.

The next morning, I put on my smartest clothes and my Sunday shoes—the ones that look professional but hurt with every step—and walked the two miles to the embassy, carrying all my documents, carrying two years of waiting, carrying the terror of what might be happening to Mike while I couldn't reach him.

I waited in line. They took my letter. They disappeared with it.

When they returned, they told me there had been an administrative error. My interview was supposed to be in London.

I used every technique I had. I breathed. I grounded myself. I stayed as calm as I could while I begged them to see me anyway. Please. I've come so far. My husband is in hospital. Please.

They agreed.

They took everything from me, including my phone. For five hours, I sat in that embassy with no way to check on Mike. No way to know if he'd had another seizure. No way to tell him where I was if he needed me.

I felt myself drowning. The fear was a physical weight on my chest. All I could think was, *What if he needs me? What if something's happening right now and I don't know?*

So I used everything I knew.

I breathed—slowly, deliberately, counting each exhale. I grounded myself—feeling my feet on the floor, the chair beneath me, the present moment. I used the container technique—taking the catastrophic images and placing them somewhere secure, telling myself *I'll deal with this later; right now, I need to be here.* I visualized the interview going smoothly. I connected with a future version of myself who had already made it through this day.

And I separated fear from reality. Yes, something could be happening to Mike, but it also might not be. The hospital had him. He was in professional care. My fear was real, but it wasn't necessarily true. Panicking wouldn't help him. Getting through this interview would.

Interestingly, I'd been anticipating a challenging interview. I'd worked myself up about how difficult it would be. How they might catch me out. How much was at stake. That was catastrophizing. And when the interview finally happened, it was absolutely fine. Almost easy. The terror I'd carried had been far worse than the reality.

When I finally walked out of the embassy, approved, I burst into tears. All the fear and emotion I'd been containing came flooding out. People stared at me—this woman sobbing on the street in her smart clothes and her hurting shoes. I didn't care.

I called Mike. He was fine. Thank God. He'd been sleeping, recovering, watched over by nurses who didn't speak his language but took good care of him anyway.

We all lived to enjoy another day.

I tell you this story not because I handled it perfectly—I didn't—but because I want you to know that these techniques work in real life, under real pressure, when everything is falling apart. Not just in quiet meditation rooms or therapy sessions, but in embassy waiting rooms and hospital corridors and the absolute chaos of life.

And I want you to know that even someone who teaches this work, who has practiced it for years, still has to consciously reach for these tools. Still feels the fear. Still has moments of drowning before finding the surface again.

That's not failure. That's being human.

The goal isn't to never feel afraid, or overwhelmed, or close to breaking. The goal is to have resources to reach for when you do. To have techniques that can help you come back to yourself, even in the storm.

You're building those resources now.

A GENTLE INVITATION

Your Practice Plan

Choose one technique from this chapter to practice this week:

Future Self-Visualization — meeting the woman who made it through

The Container — learning to park what you can't process yet

Separating Fear from Reality — questioning the stories fear tells

Self-Hypnosis — using the guide in the appendix to learn the basics

Practice when you're calm so the technique becomes familiar before you need it urgently. These skills are built with repetition—each time you practice, you're strengthening a pathway that will be there when you need it most.

Your mind is not your enemy. It may feel like it sometimes—racing with worries, replaying worst-case scenarios, refusing to give you peace. But it's also capable of creating profound calm. Of accessing wisdom. Of imagining futures that pull you forward.

The techniques in this chapter are ways of working *with* your mind rather than against it. Of using its power deliberately, instead of being used by it.

This is learnable. You don't need to be special or talented or spiritually advanced. You just need to practice. To be patient with yourself. To show up, again and again, even when it feels awkward or difficult or like nothing is happening.

Something is happening. Even when you can't see it yet.

In the next chapter, we'll turn to something that overwhelmed women often struggle with most: the radical act of boundaries. Setting limits. Saying no. Protecting your capacity.

But for now, stay with what you've learned here. Practice one technique. Notice what shifts.

You're reclaiming your mind, one practice at a time.

Chapter Nine

The Radical Act of Boundaries

I need to tell you something, and I need you to really hear it:

You are allowed to say no.

You are allowed to protect your time, your energy, your capacity. You are allowed to disappoint people. You are allowed to put yourself on your own list of people you take care of—and not at the bottom.

I know. It doesn't feel allowed. It feels selfish, unkind, wrong. It feels like something other women might be able to do, but not you. Not with your responsibilities, your relationships, your history.

But here's what I've learned, the hard way: Boundaries aren't selfish. They're survival. And without them, you will keep giving until there's nothing left—and then you won't be any good to anyone, including yourself.

This chapter is about the radical act of setting limits. Of saying no. Of protecting your capacity fiercely enough that you actually have something left to give to the things that matter most.

It's also about the guilt. Because I know the guilt is coming, and I want to help you face it.

What Boundaries Actually Are

Boundaries aren't walls. They're not about shutting people out or becoming cold and unavailable. They're about knowing where you end, and other people begin. About being clear on what you're responsible for and what you're not. About protecting the resources—time, energy, emotional capacity—that allow you to function.

Think of boundaries like the fence around a garden. The fence isn't hostile. It's not rejecting the outside world. It's simply defining a space. This is the garden. This is where things are cultivated and protected. This is what I'm tending. Without the fence, everything gets trampled. The garden can't grow.

You are the garden. And right now, you probably don't have much of a fence.

Boundaries can be:

Physical — who can touch you, how close people can stand, your need for personal space and privacy.

Emotional — how much of other people's feelings you take on, what emotional labor you're willing to do, protecting yourself from other people's negativity or criticism.

Time-based — how many hours you work, whether you answer emails at night, protecting weekends or evenings or mornings for yourself.

Energy-based — recognizing that some people and activities drain you, and limiting your exposure. Protecting your capacity for the things that matter.

Material — your money, your possessions, what you're willing to lend or give, what's yours.

Most overwhelmed women are running boundary deficits in multiple areas. The work bleeds into evenings. Other people's emotions become their responsibility. They give and give until they're empty, then feel guilty for having nothing left.

Does any of this sound familiar?

How We Learned to Have No Boundaries

If you struggle with boundaries, you probably learned to struggle with them early.

Maybe you grew up in a home where your needs were secondary to someone else's—a demanding parent, a troubled sibling, a family system that required you to be the easy one, the helpful one, the one who didn't cause problems.

Maybe you learned that saying no led to punishment, withdrawal of love, or conflict that felt unbearable. So you learned to say yes. Always yes. Yes became your survival strategy.

Maybe you absorbed the cultural message that good women are selfless. That putting yourself first is selfish. That your worth comes from what you do for others, not from who you are.

Or maybe you learned that love had to be earned through performance. That if you just did enough, gave enough, and were enough, then finally—finally—you'd be loved the way you needed to be.

I know this pattern intimately. I grew up as a people-pleaser, shaped by a difficult childhood into someone who believed that my job was to make other people happy. That their needs mattered more than mine. That if I could just get it right—be helpful enough, good enough, generous enough—I'd finally earn the love and approval I craved.

Spoiler: It never works.

I remember organizing my parents' golden wedding anniversary party. I poured everything into it—money I could barely afford, time I didn't have, emotional energy I was running low on. I just wanted them to be happy. I just wanted, if I'm honest, for them to love me.

Afterwards, my mother looked at me with scorn in her eyes. "Oh, you are *such* a Lady Bountiful," she said. Not with gratitude. With contempt.

I was crushed. All that effort, all that giving, and what I got back was criticism. It took me a long time to understand what that moment was really teaching me: that I needed boundaries not just with colleagues and clients, but with *family*. That the people we most want to please are often the ones we most need to protect ourselves from.

Family boundaries are the hardest. These are the people who installed your buttons—they know exactly where to push. They have decades of history with the old you, the compliant you, the you who always said yes. They don't like the new fence around the garden. It gets in their way.

But I learned—am still learning—that boundaries with family are not betrayal. They're self-preservation. And sometimes they're the only way the relationship can survive at all.

The Guilt (Let's Talk About It)

Here's what happens when you start setting boundaries: You feel guilty.

Horribly, painfully, almost unbearably guilty. Like you've done something wrong. Like you're a bad person. Like the discomfort of the guilt is worse than the exhaustion of having no boundaries at all.

I want to tell you something important about this guilt: **It's a sign that you're changing, not a sign that you're wrong.**

Guilt is what happens when your behavior conflicts with your beliefs. For years, maybe decades, you've believed that good people say yes, that setting limits is selfish, and that you should always put others first. When you start acting differently, your old beliefs push back. They create guilt as a warning signal: *Danger! You're doing something bad!*

But the beliefs are wrong. And the guilt, while real and painful, is not a reliable guide to whether you're actually doing something harmful.

Ask yourself, if your best friend set this boundary, would you think she was a bad person? If your daughter told you she'd said no to something that was draining her, would you be disappointed in her? Or would you be proud?

The guilt will come. Expect it. Feel it. And then do the boundaried thing anyway.

Here's what I've discovered: The guilt fades. Not immediately—it takes time and practice. But as you set boundaries and see that the world doesn't end, that relationships can survive your no, and that you actually have more to give when you're not depleted, the guilt loses its power. It becomes background noise rather than a siren.

And something unexpected often happens: Boundaries create freedom. When you know you can say no, you can say yes more wholeheartedly. When you protect your capacity, you have more to offer. When you stop resenting people for taking too much, you can actually enjoy them again.

Boundaries don't just protect you. Strangely, they release you.

Finding the Words

One of the hardest things about setting boundaries is knowing what to actually say. The words get stuck. You freeze, default to yes, and kick yourself afterwards.

So here are some scripts. Real words you can use, adapted to your situation. Practice them until they feel more natural. Have them ready before you need them.

WORDS THAT WORK

Ways to Say No

"I'd love to help, but I can't take that on right now."

"That doesn't work for me." (No explanation needed.)

"I'm not available for that."

"I need to check my calendar and get back to you." (This buys you time to decide without pressure.)

"I've got too much on my plate right now."

"I'm going to have to pass on this one."

"No." (It's a complete sentence.)

WORDS THAT WORK

Buying Time to Decide

"Can I think about it and let you know?"

"I need to look at my commitments before I can answer."

"I'm not sure. Let me get back to you tomorrow."

"I have a policy of not committing to things immediately. Can I let you know by [day]?"

WORDS THAT WORK

Setting Limits on Time and Energy

"I can give you twenty minutes, but then I need to go."

"I don't take work calls after 6 p.m."

"I'm not able to discuss this right now. Can we talk about it another time?"

"I need some time to myself this weekend."

WORDS THAT WORK

Protecting Emotional Energy

"I care about you, but I'm not the right person to help with this."

"I don't have the capacity to take this on right now."

"I'm finding this conversation difficult. I need to step away."

"I love you, and I'm not willing to discuss this topic."

Notice something about these scripts? Most of them don't include lengthy explanations or justifications. You don't have to defend your boundaries. You don't have to provide a reason that's good enough for the other person to accept. "No" is a complete sentence, and "That doesn't work for me" is a complete explanation.

The more you explain, the more you open yourself up to negotiation and pushback. Keep it simple. Keep it kind. Keep it firm.

SHE CRIED TOO

Shonda Rhimes

"I had to learn that 'No' is a complete sentence. I had to learn that I was allowed to protect my time and my peace. That wasn't selfish—that was survival."

Shonda Rhimes—creator of *Grey's Anatomy*, *Scandal*, and *How to Get Away with Murder*—wrote a book called *Year of Yes* about the year she decided to say yes to things that scared her. But what she discovered was that saying yes to the right things required learning to say no to the wrong ones. She'd been working herself into exhaustion, saying yes to every demand, every request, and every obligation. Her Year of Yes was really about learning what deserved her yes and fiercely protecting her energy from everything that didn't. She writes about the guilt, the fear of disappointing people, and the revolutionary discovery that she could set boundaries and still be loved.

When People Don't Like Your Boundaries

Here's the uncomfortable truth: Some people won't like your new boundaries. They've been benefiting from your lack of them. They've gotten used to you always saying yes, always being available, and always putting their needs first. Your boundaries inconvenience them.

And they may push back.

They might guilt-trip you: *"I thought you cared about me." "After everything I've done for you." "You've changed."*

They might get angry: *"This is ridiculous." "You're being selfish." "Who do you think you are?"*

They might try to negotiate: *"Just this once." "It won't take long." "Can't you make an exception?"*

They might withdraw: sulking or punishing you with silence.

This is hard. Really hard. Especially when it's family, or close friends, or people you love and don't want to hurt.

But here's what I want you to remember: **How someone responds to your boundary tells you something important about the relationship.**

People who respect you will respect your boundaries even if they're initially surprised or disappointed. They'll adjust. They'll accept that you're a person with limits, not an endless resource to be tapped.

People who only value you for what you give them will resist your boundaries. They'll push back, manipulate, and try to make you feel guilty. Because your boundaries threaten something they want to keep: unlimited access to your time, energy, and compliance.

This is painful information to receive. But it's also clarifying. It shows you which relationships are built on genuine mutual care and which are built on your self-abandonment.

Some relationships will improve when you set boundaries. Paradoxically, resentment lifts when you stop over-giving. You can be more present when you're not depleted. Honesty about your limits creates space for genuine connection rather than exhausted performance.

Some relationships will struggle. They may need renegotiation, difficult conversations, and a new way of being together that accommodates your humanity.

And some relationships may not survive your boundaries. This is the hardest thing to accept. But a relationship that requires your self-destruction to continue is not a relationship worth preserving.

Holding the Line

Setting a boundary is one thing. Maintaining it is another.

People will test your boundaries. They'll see if you really mean it. They'll push a little, and if you cave, they'll push more. This isn't necessarily malicious—it's just human. We all test limits to see where the edges really are.

So when someone pushes back against your boundary, you have a choice. You can hold the line—calmly, firmly, without excessive explanation—or you can cave and teach them that your boundaries don't really mean anything.

Holding the line might sound like:

"I understand you're disappointed, and my answer is still no."

"I can see this is frustrating for you. I'm still not able to do that."

"I've already answered that question. I'm not going to discuss it further."

"I love you, and this boundary isn't negotiable."

Notice the pattern: Acknowledge their feeling, then restate the boundary. You don't have to be cold or cruel. You can be warm and boundaried at the same time. In fact, that combination is the goal.

It gets easier with practice. The first few times feel excruciating. The guilt is loud, the fear of conflict is intense, and the old patterns scream at you to cave. But every time you hold the line, you build the muscle. You prove to yourself that you can do this. And you teach others that your boundaries are real.

A GENTLE INVITATION

Your Boundary Audit

Consider these questions honestly:

Where in your life are you saying yes when you mean no?

Who consistently takes more than they give?

What activities drain you, but you keep doing out of obligation?

Where do you need more protection for your time? Your energy? Your emotional capacity?

Choose one area where you want to set a firmer boundary. Just one. Start there. Practice the words. Expect the guilt. Hold the line anyway.

Boundaries are not about building walls between yourself and the world. They're about knowing your own limits and honoring them. About recognizing that you are a finite resource—your time is limited, your energy is limited, your emotional capacity is limited—and treating those limits as real rather than pretending they don't exist.

This is one of the most important lessons I've learned in my own life and one of the hardest to practice consistently. I still catch myself over-committing. I still feel the pull of people-pleasing, the old programming that tells me to say yes, to make people happy, and to earn love through giving.

But I also know, now, that this path leads nowhere good. That the resentment builds. That the depletion catches up. That the relationships I most want to protect are the ones most damaged by my inability to protect myself.

Setting boundaries is a radical act. It's radical because it goes against so much of what we've been taught about being a good woman, a good mother, a good friend, and a good employee. It's radical because it says, "I matter too. My needs are real. My limits are valid."

And it's an act—something you have to keep doing, again and again, choice by choice. Not something you achieve once and then it's done. A practice, not a destination.

In the next chapter, we'll talk about finding your people—the difference between connections that drain you and support that sustains you. Because boundaries aren't just about what you keep out; they're about creating space for what truly nourishes.

But for now, I'll leave you with this:

Every time you say no to something that depletes you, you're saying yes to something else—your health, your peace, your capacity to show up fully for the things that matter most.

That's not selfish.

That's wisdom.

Chapter Ten

Finding Your People

You can be surrounded by people and still be completely alone.

You can have a partner, children, colleagues, neighbors, a full social calendar and still feel like no one truly sees you. Like you're performing a version of yourself for an audience that doesn't know the real you exists. Like you could disappear and no one would notice the you that's actually gone, just the role you played.

This kind of loneliness is particularly cruel because it's invisible. From the outside, your life looks full of connection. You're not the obvious picture of isolation—you're not living alone with no one to talk to. So you feel like you can't complain. You feel like something must be wrong with you for feeling lonely when you have all these people around.

But loneliness isn't about the number of people in your life. It's about whether any of them truly know you. Whether you can be yourself—your real, messy, struggling self—and still be accepted.

Whether there's anyone you can call at 2 a.m. when everything falls apart.

This chapter is about finding your people. Not collecting acquaintances or building a bigger network, but cultivating the kind of connections that actually sustain you. The relationships that fill your cup rather than drain it. The people who see you clearly and love you anyway.

Because here's what I've learned: You can't do this alone. We're not designed to. And trying to carry everything by yourself, never letting anyone see you struggle, is part of how many of us ended up crying in the shower in the first place.

The Loneliness No One Talks About

We're in the middle of a loneliness epidemic, and women are not immune. Despite social media connecting us to hundreds of friends. Despite busy lives full of interactions. Despite being constantly available via text and email and video call, many women report feeling more isolated than ever.

Part of this is the nature of modern life. We've lost the villages, the extended families living nearby, the natural communities that used to form around neighborhoods and churches and shared daily life. We've gained independence and mobility, but we've lost the web of connection that used to catch us when we fell.

Part of it is the performance of social media, where we show highlight reels and hide the struggles. It's hard to feel connected when everyone's pretending to be fine. And it's hard to admit you're struggling when everyone else seems to have it together.

And part of it is just being too busy and too depleted to invest in relationships. Friendship takes time and energy—two things overwhelmed women have in desperately short supply. So connections become transactional, surface-level, and limited to the quick chat at school pickup or the brief exchange with colleagues. Not the deep, nourishing relationships we actually need.

Loneliness can exist anywhere. Inside a marriage, where you sleep next to someone every night but feel like strangers. Inside a family, where you're surrounded by people who need you but don't really see you. Inside a workplace, where you're collegial and friendly, but no one knows what's actually going on in your life.

If you recognize this feeling, please know: There's nothing wrong with you. You're experiencing something millions of women experience. The hunger for real connection is not a character flaw—it's a human need.

Bloom Where You're Planted (Even When the Soil Is Rocky)

There's a particular kind of loneliness that comes with being transplanted—whether across the world, across the country, or even just to a new town where you don't know anyone. You've left behind the people who knew you, the places that felt like home, the shorthand of old friendships where you didn't have to explain yourself. And you've landed somewhere new, where you have to start from scratch.

I know this loneliness intimately.

I'm English. I lived in England and Europe for sixty years, with a brief stay in Alaska, before I immigrated to the United States on Valentine's Day 2019. I followed every proper procedure—which was onerous, to say the least—and became a US citizen in 2023. I'm as American as the law can make me.

But I still have a British accent. After sixty-plus years of being a Brit, that's not going to change. I still use British vocabulary that sometimes confuses people or marks me as different. I've tried hard to modify my language, but I still stick out.

Some people like it. Others... not so much. There's a particular look I've learned to recognize: *Who is SHE to have opinions?* The suspicion of the outsider.

Kentucky, where I live now, is a beautiful place with many warm people. But it's also old-fashioned in ways that can make fitting in challenging. I've been made to feel welcome, but often at arm's length. The arm's-length welcome that never quite becomes an embrace. Friendly, but not quite friends. Included, but not quite belonging.

I have a fridge magnet that says, "Bloom where you are planted." I suspect many immigrants and transplants have something similar—a little reminder to make the best of where we've landed, to put down roots even in unfamiliar soil.

But sometimes the soil is rocky. Sometimes blooming takes longer than we expected. And sometimes we need to grieve what we've left behind while still trying to grow something new.

If you've been transplanted, whether by choice, by circumstance, by a partner's job, or by necessity, I see you. Building community from scratch is exhausting work. Especially when you're already carrying so much else.

What I Left Behind

Before I moved to Kentucky, I lived in Wyoming for six years. When I arrived there, I was a stranger too—the English woman with the accent, the outsider trying to find her place.

It wasn't easy at first. It took time. At least three years before I truly felt I belonged.

But eventually, I found my people. We called ourselves "the gang"—eight of us, four couples who just jelled. The kind of friends where you can show up without makeup, say the wrong thing, have a bad day, and still be loved. The kind of friends who bring food when you're sick and laughter when you're sad, and honesty when you need to hear it.

Leaving them was one of the hardest parts of moving. We had good reasons to relocate—better healthcare access for my husband, and easier flights to England, where my daughters live. Good reasons. The right reasons, probably.

But I'd be lying if I said my heart didn't ache for those friends. There's a space in my life only they can fill. I love them. I miss them. And I've learned that you can't make new old friends, that the depth that comes from years of shared history can't be rushed or replicated.

I share this because I want you to know that I understand. If you're grieving connections you've lost—to distance, to circumstance, to the natural drift of life—that grief is real. It deserves acknowledgment, not dismissal.

And I share it because of what else I learned in Wyoming: It took three years. Three years of showing up, of being patient, of letting friendship develop at its own pace. Three years before those strangers became my gang.

If you're in year one of being somewhere new, hold onto that. It gets better. The soil that feels rocky now can become fertile ground. But it takes time.

SHE CRIED TOO

Glennon Doyle

"I have a few friends who fill me up, and that's enough. I used to think I needed a big squad. What I actually needed was a small circle of people who would tell me the truth and love me anyway."

Glennon Doyle—author of *Untamed* and founder of the Together Rising community—writes extensively about the power of true friendship and what she calls her "sister-friends." After years of struggling with addiction and hiding her true self, she learned that real connection requires vulnerability—showing people who you actually are, not the performance of who you think you should be. She's spoken about how her closest friendships saved her life and how she had to learn to let people in before she could experience the support she desperately needed. Her message: You don't need everyone to love you. You just need a few people who really see you.

Venting Friends vs. Growth Friends

Not all connections are created equal. And here's something important to consider: some friendships can actually keep you stuck.

You probably know what I mean. The friend who's always ready to hear about your problems—and add fuel to the fire. Who matches your complaints with their own, building a bonfire of mutual grievance. Who validates every negative feeling without ever gently suggesting that maybe, just maybe, there's another way to look at things.

Venting can feel good in the moment. There's relief in being heard, in having someone agree that yes, your boss is terrible, your partner is thoughtless, your situation is impossible. It feels like support.

But venting has a dark side. Research suggests that excessive venting—going over and over the same problems without moving toward solutions—can actually intensify negative emotions rather than releasing them. It's called "co-rumination," and it's particularly common in women's friendships. We bond over shared problems, and in doing so, we can keep each other stuck in them.

Then there's another kind of connection I've observed. The friend who loves drama, so long as it's not their own. Who seems energized by your difficulties. Who leans in when things are going wrong and drifts away when things improve.

I had a client recently who was meeting an acquaintance for lunch—someone going through significant difficulties. When I gently suggested she might not have the emotional capacity to give, given everything on her own plate, she said something that stopped me cold: *"I feel better knowing someone else has worse things to deal with."*

I understood what she meant—the relief of perspective, of realizing your problems could be worse. But there was something else there, too. A hunger for someone else's drama. A way of feeling better about her own life by comparison.

This is not support. This is spectatorship.

True support looks different. A growth friend listens to your struggles and then helps you move forward. She validates your feelings *and* gently challenges you when you're stuck. She's honest enough to tell you when you're being your own worst enemy. She believes in your capacity to grow, change, and overcome, and she reflects that belief back to you.

Growth friends don't let you wallow indefinitely. They sit with you in the darkness for a while, and then they help you find the light switch.

The future starts right here, right now. And the friends who will help you build that future are the ones who believe it's possible.

Being the Friend You Want to Have

Here's the uncomfortable flip side: If we want growth friends, we need to be growth friends.

Are you the venting friend? The one who calls to complain but never to celebrate? The one who brings problems but not solutions? The one who takes more energy than she gives?

When you're overwhelmed, it's easy to become that person. You're running on empty, so all you have to offer is your emptiness. Every conversation becomes a download of everything that's wrong. You don't mean to be draining—you're just drained.

But this is worth examining. Because friendship is reciprocal, and if all we bring is our burdens, we may find our friendships struggling to bear the weight.

I'm not saying you can't share your struggles—of course you can and should. That's what friends are for. But share forward, not just backward. Vent when you need to, then ask, *What am I going to do about this? What's my next step?* Bring your friends into your growth, not just your grievances.

And be the friend who helps others grow, too. Listen with compassion, then ask the gentle questions. *What do you think you might do? How can I support you in moving forward? What would you tell a friend in your situation?*

Be part of the solution, not part of the problem. That's how we build friendships that sustain us both.

SHE CRIED TOO

Elizabeth Gilbert

"In the midst of my divorce, I learned who my real friends were. They weren't the ones who told me what I wanted to hear. They were the ones who sat with me in my pain and then helped me find my way out."

Elizabeth Gilbert—author of *Eat, Pray, Love*—has written about how friendship sustained her through her divorce and the difficult years that followed. She learned to distinguish between friends who enabled her worst instincts and friends who loved her enough to tell her hard truths. The friends who helped her grow were the ones who could hold space for her pain without drowning in it with her, who believed she was capable of more than wallowing, even when she didn't believe it herself. Real friendship, she discovered, isn't about endless validation. It's about being seen, being held, and being gently encouraged toward your own growth.

The Loneliness Within

Some of the loneliest women I know are married.

They share a home with someone, sleep in the same bed, navigate daily life together—and feel utterly alone. Their partner doesn't really know them anymore. Doesn't ask about their inner world. Doesn't notice when they're struggling. They've become co-managers of a household, not intimate companions.

This loneliness is particularly painful because it exists in the space where connection is supposed to be. You're not alone—you have a partner, a family, people around you all the time. So the loneliness feels like a personal failure. Like you should be grateful for what you have. Like you have no right to want more.

But you do have a right to want more. To want to be seen. To want real intimacy, not just proximity. To want someone who knows the real you, not just the role you play.

If this resonates, I want to say gently: this might be territory for couples therapy, for honest conversations, for examining what's happened to the connection you once had. It's beyond the scope of this book to fix a relationship, but I want to name this loneliness, because so many women carry it silently.

And I want to say this too: Even within a marriage or family that isn't meeting your connection needs, you can build other relationships that do. You can have friends who see you. You can create spaces where you're known. Your partner doesn't have to be your everything—and expecting them to be is often part of the problem.

Finding Connection When You're Running on Empty

Here's the cruel irony: When we most need connection, we often have the least energy to build it.

Building friendships takes effort. You have to show up, make conversation, follow up, and be interested in someone else's life when you can barely manage your own. When you're overwhelmed and depleted, the thought of adding anything to your plate—even something good—feels impossible.

And so we isolate. We tell ourselves we'll reach out when we have more energy. We'll socialize when things calm down. We'll invest in friendships when we're not so busy.

But things don't calm down. And the isolation makes everything harder.

So what do you do when you need people but have no energy to find them?

Follow your passions. This is my best advice: Don't try to make friends in the abstract. Do things you actually care about, and let the friendships form naturally. Take an art class. Join a yoga studio. Find a book club. Volunteer for a cause you believe in. When you're doing something you love, you'll meet others who love it too. You'll have something to talk about beyond small talk. And showing up won't feel like such a drain because you're doing it for yourself anyway.

Start small. You don't need to build a whole community overnight. You need one conversation. One coffee. One genuine exchange with another human being. Start there. Let it build naturally.

Be honest about where you are. You don't have to pretend to be fine. When someone asks how you are, you can say, "It's been a hard season" without unloading your entire story. A little honesty invites connection in a way that "I'm fine!" never does.

Don't stay home and fear the outside. I know it feels safer to retreat. To conserve your limited energy by staying in, staying small, and staying hidden. But isolation makes depression and anxiety worse. Even small forays into the world—the farmers' market, the coffee shop, the walking trail—keep you connected to life outside your own head.

Accept that it takes time. Real friendship isn't instant. Remember: it took me three years in Wyoming before I found my gang. Give yourself permission to be in the building phase. Let relationships develop at their own pace. Don't give up just because you haven't found your people yet.

A GENTLE INVITATION

Your Connection Inventory

Consider these questions honestly:

Who in your life truly knows you—the real you, not the performance?

Who could you call at 2 a.m. if everything fell apart?

Which relationships fill your cup? Which drain it?

Are your friendships helping you grow, or keeping you stuck?

What's one thing you could do this week to nurture a real connection?

You don't need a hundred friends. You need a few real ones. Focus your limited energy there.

A Small Circle Is Enough

You don't need to be popular. You don't need a wide social circle or a packed calendar or hundreds of friends on social media.

What you need is a few people who really matter. Who know you. Who show up. Who let you be yourself.

Research on happiness and longevity consistently shows that it's not the quantity of relationships that predicts well-being—it's the quality. A handful of close, genuine connections is worth more than a hundred shallow ones.

So don't exhaust yourself trying to maintain friendships that don't nourish you. Don't say yes to social obligations that leave you emptier. Don't measure your worth by how many people like your posts or show up to your parties.

Instead, invest in the relationships that matter. Nurture the friendships where you feel seen. Give your limited energy to the people who give energy back.

A small circle of genuine connection is not a failure. It's a success.

We are not meant to do this alone. We're wired for connection—biologically, psychologically, and spiritually. And when we try to carry everything by ourselves, refusing to let anyone see our struggles, we make everything harder.

Finding your people is not a luxury. It's a necessity. Not for weakness, but for wholeness.

This might mean nurturing existing relationships that have been neglected. It might mean letting go of friendships that drain more than they give. It might mean being brave enough to reach out, show up, and let yourself be seen.

It takes time. The soil might be rocky. You might be grieving connections you've lost while trying to build new ones.

But somewhere out there are people who will love the real you—not the performance, not the people-pleaser, not the woman who says yes to everything and hides her tears in the shower. The *real* you.

Keep looking. Keep showing up. Keep being brave enough to let people in.

Your people are out there. And when you find them or when they find you, everything will feel a little more possible.

The tools are yours now. You don't have to use them perfectly — you just have to use them. And in Part Four, we talk about what it looks like to build a life where the shower is just a shower.

PART FOUR

Beyond the Shower
Building a Sustainable Life

Chapter Eleven

The Rest Revolution

I want to tell you something radical:

You don't have to earn rest.

Rest is not a reward for productivity. It's not something you deserve only after you've crossed everything off your list. It's not laziness, self-indulgence, or evidence that you're not trying hard enough.

Rest is a biological necessity. Like food, like water, like air. Your body requires it to function. And when you don't get it—when you push through, power on, and tell yourself you'll rest when you're finished—you're not being strong. You're running up a debt that will eventually be collected, with interest.

This chapter is about rest. Not the Instagram version of self-care—bubble baths and face masks and treating yourself—but the real, revolutionary act of allowing your body and mind to recover. Of stepping off the treadmill long enough to remember what it feels like to stand still.

For many of us, this is the hardest chapter in the book. Because rest requires something we struggle with deeply… permission.

The Fixer Who Couldn't Stop

I had a client recently, a kind, generous woman in her early 30s, Madeline, who was clearly running on empty. Hurt. In pain. Exhausted in ways that sleep alone couldn't fix.

I suggested a yoga retreat. Just a few days away, for herself, to gather her thoughts. To remember who she was outside all her responsibilities.

I thought I'd offered her a gift. But what I saw was panic.

She couldn't go alone. Maybe her sister could come? And her mother would love it. And she couldn't possibly leave her husband for that long. And when I suggested it could be a no-phone zone, genuine fear crossed her face.

She is the fixer, you see. She has always been the fixer. The one who holds everything together, who solves everyone's problems, and who stays connected and available in case anyone needs her.

She works in the family business—has worked there since she was young, was groomed for it since birth, and chose her degrees based on her father's suggestions. Everything she does is firefighting for other people's emergencies. At thirty-four, she's finally wondering *Who am I? Who have I ever been?*

That question is painful. And it's also the beginning.

If you see yourself in her story, I want you to know, you're not alone. So many women have built their entire identities around being needed, being useful, and being the one who copes. Rest feels dangerous because if you stop fixing, who are you?

But you are more than what you do for others. And discovering that—terrifying as it might be—is essential work.

What Happens When You Don't Rest

Let's talk science for a moment because understanding what's actually happening in your body might help you take this seriously.

Sleep isn't just rest for your muscles. It's when your brain consolidates memories, processes emotions, and clears out metabolic waste. It's when your body repairs tissue, regulates hormones, and maintains immune function. It's when the nervous system finally gets to shift from sympathetic (fight-or-flight) to parasympathetic (rest-and-restore).

When you don't get enough sleep, everything suffers. Cognitive function declines—you make more mistakes, struggle to focus, and have difficulty making decisions. Emotional regulation deteriorates—you're more reactive, more anxious, and more likely to snap. Your immune system weakens. Your metabolism changes. Your risk of heart disease, diabetes, and other chronic conditions increases.

And here's something crucial: Chronic sleep deprivation and chronic hypervigilance create a vicious cycle.

Hypervigilance is the state of being constantly alert for danger—scanning for threats, ready to respond at any moment. It's what keeps you listening for the cry of a child, waiting for the phone call from work, and bracing for the next crisis. It's useful in genuine emergencies. But when it becomes your baseline—when you're *always* on alert—it wreaks havoc on your body.

Hypervigilance keeps your sympathetic nervous system activated. Cortisol stays elevated. Your body never gets the signal that it's safe to rest. Even when you lie down to sleep, part of you is still listening, still scanning, still ready.

This is why so many overwhelmed women struggle with sleep. It's not just the busy mind—though that's real too. It's a nervous system that has forgotten how to switch off. That doesn't believe it's safe to rest. That has learned, through years of being needed, that letting down your guard is dangerous.

The result of the research is clear: Chronic hypervigilance significantly increases the risk of cardiovascular disease, autoimmune disorders, chronic pain conditions, and mental health problems. It literally damages your body over time.

This isn't weakness. This is biology. And ignoring it doesn't make you strong; it just delays the inevitable crash.

SHE CRIED TOO

Anne Lamott

"Almost everything will work again if you unplug it for a few minutes, including you."

Writer Anne Lamott is known for her candid reflections on faith, recovery, and the messy realities of being human. Through addiction, loss, and decades of writing about spiritual life, she learned that exhaustion often comes from trying to carry everything alone. Her gentle wisdom reminds us that human beings are not machines designed for endless output. Like any system under strain, we need pauses. We need stillness. And sometimes the most healing thing we can do is simply step back long enough to breathe.

Rest Is More Than Sleep

Here's something that might explain a lot: You can be getting eight hours of sleep and still be exhausted.

That's because sleep is only one type of rest, and our bodies need several different kinds to function well. Dr. Saundra Dalton-Smith, a physician and researcher, has identified seven types of rest that human beings require:

Physical rest — both passive (sleeping, napping) and active (gentle stretching, massage, restorative yoga). This is rest for your body.

Mental rest — breaks for your overworked brain. The cognitive load of holding everything together is exhausting. Mental rest means periods where you're not planning, organizing, problem-solving, or keeping track of everyone's needs.

Emotional rest — time and space to be authentic, to stop performing, to not have to manage anyone else's feelings. This is rest from the relentless emotional labor so many women carry.

Sensory rest — relief from the constant stimulation of screens, lights, noise, and information. Modern life bombards our senses constantly. Sensory rest means turning things off and letting your nervous system settle.

Creative rest — exposure to beauty and inspiration. Nature, art, music—things that fill you up rather than demand from you. Many women are so busy producing that they never receive.

Social rest — time with people who restore you rather than drain you, or time alone if that's what you need. Not all socializing is restful—some is deeply depleting.

Spiritual rest — connection to something larger than yourself. This might be religious practice, or time in nature, or meditation, or simply moments of awe and meaning. It's rest for your soul.

Of all the types of rest we've discussed, spiritual rest deserves a little more attention—because for many women, it's the foundation that makes all the other rest possible.

I want to tread gently here. Faith and spirituality are deeply personal. Some of you reading this have a strong religious faith that anchors your life. Some of you are spiritual but not religious. Some of you aren't sure what you believe. And some of you have been wounded by religion or find the whole topic uncomfortable.

All of that is okay. This isn't about telling you what to believe. It's about acknowledging something that research—and lived experience—consistently shows: Connection to something larger than ourselves is good for our mental health.

Study after study confirms what many women know intuitively: Those who have some form of spiritual or faith practice tend to experience lower rates of depression and anxiety, greater resilience in the face of hardship, a stronger sense of meaning and purpose, and better overall well-being. This holds true across different religions and different forms of spirituality.

Why might this be? Several reasons seem to matter:

A sense of meaning. When life is hard—and it often is—believing that our struggles have purpose, that we're part of something bigger than our individual circumstances, can make the unbearable more bearable. It doesn't make pain disappear, but it can make it feel less random, less pointless.

The comfort of not being alone. Whether you call it God, the Universe, Source, Higher Power, or something else entirely—the sense that something greater is with you, that you're held even when you feel like you're falling, is profoundly comforting. Many women describe feeling accompanied, watched over, and loved by something beyond the human relationships in their lives.

Permission to surrender control. So much of our overwhelm comes from trying to control things we cannot control. Faith—in whatever form—often involves a practice of release. Of acknowledging that we cannot manage everything, that some things must be entrusted to something larger. This surrender isn't giving up; it's wisdom. It's the serenity prayer in action—accepting what we cannot change.

Built-in practices that calm the nervous system. Prayer, meditation, chanting, yoga, contemplative reading, sitting in silence—these practices that are woven through various faith traditions aren't just spiritually meaningful. They're physiologically regulating. They activate the parasympathetic nervous system. They calm the body and quiet the mind. Whether you're praying the rosary, practicing mindfulness meditation, moving through yoga asanas, or sitting in Quaker silence, you're giving your nervous system a rest.

Community. Faith traditions often come with built-in community—people who show up when you're struggling, who bring meals when you're ill, and who pray for you when you can't find the words yourself. This isn't true of all spiritual paths, but for many women, their faith community is their primary source of support and connection.

What I've Found

I'll share my own experience, not to prescribe anything, but to open a door.

I find comfort in feeling that I'm part of a bigger plan. That the struggles and joys of my life aren't random, but woven into something meaningful that I may not fully understand from where I stand. This doesn't mean I think everything happens for a reason in some tidy way—I've experienced too much suffering to believe in easy explanations. But I do feel held by something larger than myself, and that holding has gotten me through dark nights I'm not sure I could have survived alone.

I find prayer helpful—not always as a request for intervention, but as a conversation, a way of not being alone with my thoughts and fears. I find meditation helpful—the simple practice of sitting in stillness and letting thoughts pass like clouds. I find yoga helpful—the way movement and breath together become a kind of embodied prayer, a way of being present in my body instead of trapped in my anxious mind.

These practices don't make life easy. They don't prevent overwhelm or guarantee peace. But they give me somewhere to go when I'm struggling. They remind me that I'm not carrying everything alone. They rest something deep in my soul that no amount of sleep or bubble baths can touch.

An Invitation, Not a Prescription

If you already have a faith or spiritual practice, I want to encourage you: lean into it. Don't let it be the first thing you drop when life gets busy. It may be the very thing that sustains you through the busy seasons. The comfort you find there is real.

The peace is real. The research backs up what you already know in your heart.

If you've drifted from a faith that once nourished you, perhaps this is a gentle invitation to explore returning—not out of obligation or guilt, but because you deserve the comfort it once gave you.

If you've never had a faith practice but feel curious, there are so many paths to explore. You might try meditation—there are countless apps and approaches, from secular mindfulness to practices rooted in Buddhist, Christian, or other traditions. You might try yoga—not just as exercise, but as a contemplative practice. You might explore a faith community and see if it resonates. You might simply start spending time in nature with an attitude of openness and wonder, noticing what happens when you quiet yourself enough to listen.

And if spirituality isn't your path—if you've thoughtfully concluded that this isn't for you—that's okay too. There's no judgment here. The other six types of rest are still available to you, and many people live meaningful, resilient lives without traditional faith. This section is for those who might find comfort here, not a prescription for everyone.

What matters is that you find what genuinely rests your soul—whatever that looks like for you.

We are small creatures in a vast universe, carrying burdens that sometimes feel far too heavy for our human shoulders. The relief of feeling that we're not alone in this—that something larger holds us, sees us, walks with us—is a rest that goes deeper than any other.

Whether you find that rest in a church pew, a meditation cushion, a yoga mat, a walk in the woods, or the quiet of your own heart—may you find it. May you rest there. And may you rise from that rest a little more whole.

Most overwhelmed women are running deficits in multiple areas. You might be sleeping but never getting mental rest. You might be around people constantly but never get emotional rest. You might be on holiday, but scrolling on your phone, missing the sensory rest your nervous system craves.

Understanding this can help you identify what kind of rest you most need—and why eight hours of sleep isn't solving the problem.

Why We Can't Give Ourselves Permission

If rest is so essential, why do we resist it so fiercely?

Part of it is practical. The demands are real. The to-do list doesn't disappear just because you're tired. The children still need feeding, the work still needs doing—the responsibilities don't pause just because you're depleted.

But part of it is deeper. It's the belief that rest must be earned. That we're only allowed to stop when everything is done, which, of course, means never. That resting when there's work to be done is lazy, selfish, and wrong.

It's the fear of what people will think. That we'll be seen as not coping, not managing, and not pulling our weight. That we'll be judged as weak, as uncommitted, as *less than.*

It's the identity we've built around being the strong one. If we rest, if we admit we're tired, if we let anyone see that we're struggling, who are we then? Some of us would rather collapse than admit we need to sit down.

And sometimes it's the assumption that others can't cope without us. That everything will fall apart if we step away. That we're so essential, so indispensable, that the world can't manage without our constant attention.

This is both a burden and, if we're honest, sometimes a form of pride. We tell ourselves we can't rest because we're needed. But perhaps we also don't *want* to discover that things can manage without us. Perhaps we've confused being needed with being worthy.

Rest as Resistance

Here's a reframe that might help: In a culture that values productivity above all else, choosing rest is a radical act.

We live in a society that profits from our exhaustion. That sells you energy drinks and productivity apps, and the myth of having it all. That measures your worth by your output. That calls rest “lazy” and busyness “success.”

Choosing to rest anyway is resistance. It's a refusal to be used up. It's a declaration that your value exists beyond what you produce.

This might feel dramatic. It's not. Every time you push through when you need to stop, you're complying with a system that treats people as resources to be depleted. Every time you rest when you “shouldn't,” you're quietly insisting on your own wholeness.

This isn't about being unproductive or abandoning your responsibilities. It's about refusing to sacrifice your health, your sanity, your *self* on the altar of getting things done.

SHE CRIED TOO

Audre Lorde

"Caring for myself is not self-indulgence, it is self-preservation, and that is an act of political warfare."

Audre Lorde was a poet, activist, and self-described "Black, lesbian, mother, warrior, poet." She lived with cancer for fourteen years while continuing to write, teach, and fight for justice. She understood that the systems she was fighting against would happily consume her entirely—and that refusing to be consumed was itself a form of resistance. Her words have become a touchstone for anyone struggling to justify taking care of themselves in a world that demands their constant sacrifice. Self-care, she taught, isn't selfish. It's how we survive long enough to do the work that matters.

When the Body Forces the Issue

If you won't choose rest, your body will eventually choose it for you.

I learned this the hard way, years ago, when I ended up in hospital with pancreatitis. My body had been sending me signals for a while—the whisperings that something wasn't right, the symptoms I kept pushing aside because I didn't have time to deal with them. I told myself I'd see a doctor when things calmed down. I told myself it probably wasn't serious. I told myself I couldn't afford to be ill.

And then I was in a hospital bed, with no choice in the matter.

This is a pattern I see constantly. Women ignore their bodies' signals because they can't face the consequences. They deny there's a problem because acknowledging it would mean having to stop. They're terrified of being "down for recovery" or "out of service"—as if they're machines rather than human beings.

But here's what I learned in that hospital bed: A forced stop is so much harder than a chosen pause.

When you choose to rest—even when it's inconvenient, even when it feels impossible—you have some control. You can plan for it, communicate about it, and manage the transition. When your body forces rest upon you, you have none. Everything you were holding collapses at once.

And here's the other thing I learned: everything managed without me. The world didn't end. The people who needed me... coped. Some of them even rose to the occasion in ways I wouldn't have predicted.

Which leads me to something important:

The Gift of Being Cared For

One of the hidden costs of being the strong one, the fixer, the one who copes: you never let anyone take care of you.

You're so busy being needed that you forget how to need. You assume others can't cope, so you never give them the chance to try. You protect everyone from having to step up and in doing so, you rob them of the opportunity to grow, to contribute, to experience the satisfaction of being helpful.

And you rob yourself of something precious: the experience of being held.

Allowing someone else to care for you is an act of trust. It's vulnerability. It's letting go of control. And yes, it's scary—especially if you've learned that depending on others leads to disappointment.

But it's also connective. When you let someone care for you, you're inviting them into a deeper relationship. You're saying, "I trust you. I need you. I'm not just here to give; I'm here to receive too."

This matters for your relationships. Partners, children, friends—they need to be needed too. When you do everything yourself, you inadvertently communicate that they're not capable, not trusted, not necessary. Letting them step up when you step back creates balance. It strengthens bonds. It teaches children that it's okay to be human, to struggle, to need help sometimes.

The message you're modeling matters. If your children watch you run yourself into the ground and never rest, what are they learning? That self-destruction is admirable? That asking for help is shameful? That their worth depends on their productivity?

Or they could learn something different. They could learn that it's okay to be down for a bit. That strong people rest. That receiving care is as valuable as giving it.

What do you want to teach them?

Rest in the Real World

All this philosophy is well and good, but what does rest actually look like when you have no time?

Let's be practical.

Micro-rest. You might not have hours, but you have moments. Five minutes of sitting with your eyes closed. One deep breath before answering the phone. A pause between tasks where you do nothing—nothing at all—for sixty seconds. These micro-doses of rest add up, and they teach your nervous system that pausing is allowed.

Protect the transitions. The spaces between activities are often where rest can hide. The commute home. The walk from your car to the building. The time after the kids are in bed. Guard these transitions. Don't fill them with more stimulation. Let them be empty. Let them rest.

Create no-phone zones. Remember my client who panicked at this suggestion? Our phones keep us hypervigilant—always available, always checking, always ready to respond to the next demand. Designating times or spaces where the phone stays off (or in another room) is one of the most effective ways to give your nervous system a break.

Schedule rest like an appointment. If it's not in the calendar, it won't happen. Block time for rest the way you'd block time for a meeting. Treat it as non-negotiable. You wouldn't cancel a doctor's appointment because someone needed something from you. Don't cancel your rest either.

Lower the bar. Rest doesn't have to look like a spa retreat or a week at the beach. It can be ten minutes on the porch. An evening where you do nothing productive. A morning where you don't set an alarm. Start where you are, with what you have.

Identify your rest language. What actually restores you? For some people, it's solitude and silence. For others, it's gentle movement or time in nature or being with one close friend. Know what fills your cup, specifically, and prioritize that over generic self-care advice that might not fit you.

A GENTLE INVITATION

Your Rest Audit

Consider the seven types of rest. Where are your biggest deficits?

Physical rest: Are you getting enough sleep? Does your body feel rested?

Mental rest: Does your brain ever get a break from planning and problem-solving?

Emotional rest: Do you have space to be authentic, or are you always performing?

Sensory rest: How much screen time and stimulation are you taking in?

Creative rest: When did you last experience beauty or inspiration?

Social rest: Are your relationships restoring you or depleting you?

Spiritual rest: Do you feel connected to something larger than your to-do list?

Choose one type of rest to focus on this week. Just one. What's one small thing you could do to address that deficit?

Rest is not weakness. Rest is not laziness. Rest is not something you earn by working yourself to exhaustion.

Rest is a biological necessity, a revolutionary act, and—perhaps most importantly—a form of self-respect.

When you rest, you're declaring that you matter. That your health matters. That your well-being is not negotiable, not something to be sacrificed on the altar of productivity or other people's needs.

I know it's hard. I know the guilt is loud. I know the demands are real and the time is short, and everyone needs something from you.

But you cannot pour from an empty cup. And if you don't choose rest, eventually your body will choose it for you—in a hospital bed, or a breakdown, or an illness that stops you in your tracks.

A chosen pause is always gentler than a forced stop.

So rest. Even when it's inconvenient. Even when it feels impossible. Even when every fiber of your being is screaming that you should be doing something productive.

Rest anyway.

It might be the bravest thing you do.

Chapter Twelve

Letting Go of Perfect

I need to tell you something about perfectionism:

It's not about having high standards. It's not about excellence or quality or doing your best. Those are good things.

Perfectionism is armor. It's the belief that if you do everything perfectly, you can avoid criticism, rejection, and shame. If you never make a mistake, no one can hurt you. If you control every detail, you'll finally be safe.

It's an exhausting way to live. And it doesn't work.

This chapter is about recognizing perfectionism for what it really is—not a virtue but a prison. And beginning the work of letting good enough be enough.

Where Perfectionism Comes From

Nobody is born a perfectionist. We learn it.

Sometimes we learn it from critical parents, teachers, or others who made us feel that mistakes were unacceptable. That anything less than perfect would be punished, mocked, or met with disappointment.

Sometimes we learn it from conditional love—the message that we're only valuable when we achieve, perform, succeed. That love must be earned through being exceptional.

Sometimes we learn it from chaos—growing up in unpredictable environments where controlling what we could control felt like the only way to survive. If I can just get this perfect, maybe everything will be okay.

And sometimes we learn it from trauma. Clinicians increasingly recognize that obsessive perfectionism and some forms of OCD can be expressions of underlying trauma—the desperate attempt to control an uncontrollable world. *If I check everything, organize everything, perfect everything, maybe I'll be safe. Maybe I'll be enough. Maybe someone will love me.*

The root of perfectionism is almost always fear. Fear of not being good enough. Fear of judgment. Fear of being seen as we really are and found wanting.

When you understand this, you can begin to have compassion for your perfectionist self. She's not trying to be difficult or controlling or impossible to please. She's trying to protect you from pain.

The problem is, the protection has become its own kind of prison.

The Impossible Tightrope

I learned perfectionism early, though it took me years to recognize what I'd learned.

Growing up, I was athletic and academic—good at school, good at sports, capable of winning. But winning wasn't celebrated in my family. When I came top in a test or won a race, I was told I was "showing off." My parents never came to my sports events. Excellence was met with suspicion, as if succeeding meant I thought I was better than I should be.

"You're no better than you should be, Jill," my mother would say—an English phrase I never fully understood, but felt in my bones. It meant: Don't get above yourself. Don't shine too brightly. Who do you think you are?

But coming fourth or worse? That attracted criticism for not studying hard enough, not practicing enough, and not trying.

So I perfected the art of coming second or third.

This is actually much harder than winning or failing. It requires constant calibration. You have to do well enough to avoid criticism but not so well that you attract the accusation of showing off. You have to succeed just the right amount—never too much, never too little.

It's an impossible tightrope. And walking it became second nature.

When I earned a place at a top school, based on a high IQ and general knowledge entrance exam, I was not congratulated. Instead, I was told that I'd done it to make my sister feel bad, she is younger than me and I guess my parents thought that I was setting too high a bar for my sister who was less academic than me, though excellent at other things. (She failed the same exam a couple of years later.) My achievement was reframed as cruelty, as boasting, as proof of some character flaw.

What do you do with that? You learn that succeeding is dangerous. You learn to dim your light. You learn that being too good at anything will be punished. And you develop an exquisitely tuned perfectionism that's actually about being just imperfect enough to be safe.

If any of this resonates—if you learned that excellence was threatening, that success was showing off, that being too good at anything made you a target—I see you. The tightrope you've been walking is exhausting. And it's time to step off.

SHE CRIED TOO

Maya Angelou

"We delight in the beauty of the butterfly, but rarely admit the changes it has gone through to achieve that beauty."

Maya Angelou—poet, memoirist, civil rights activist, and one of the most celebrated voices in American literature—lived a life that looked, from the outside, like an extraordinary series of achievements. What she wrote about, honestly and unflinchingly, was the interior journey: the shame, the silence, the years of not feeling enough. She experienced trauma, poverty, and marginalization, and yet she never presented herself as someone who had transcended all of that cleanly and completely.

She spoke about the ongoing work of becoming—of refusing to let the world's judgment become her own inner voice, of choosing to keep going even when "going" looked nothing like the polished version the world preferred to see. Her message was never *I have arrived.* It was *I kept going anyway.* That distinction matters enormously for women who feel they should have it together by now—who look at what they've achieved and still can't shake the sense that they're not quite enough.

Perfectionism, Angelou understood, is about the gap between who we are and who we think we should be by now. The butterfly metaphor cuts right to the heart of it: We celebrate the result and erase the struggle. This book refuses to do that. The struggle is the point. The struggle is where the transformation actually happens.

What Perfectionism Actually Costs

Perfectionism might feel like it's serving you—keeping your standards high, motivating you to do your best. But it's costing you more than you probably realize.

Procrastination. This seems paradoxical—perfectionists should be super productive, right? But often the opposite is true. When the standard is perfection, starting anything becomes terrifying. What if it's not good enough? What if I fail? Better to not start at all than to produce something imperfect. So tasks get delayed, projects stall, and the perfectionist berates herself for not getting things done—adding more shame to the pile.

Paralysis. Even when you do start, perfectionism can freeze you in place. Every decision feels monumental because any choice might be wrong. You get stuck in endless research, revision, and second-guessing. The fear of making a mistake makes it impossible to move forward.

Never finishing. Because nothing is ever perfect enough, projects never feel complete. There's always one more thing to fix, one more revision to make, one more way it could be better. Things sit at 95 percent done forever because that last 5 percent would mean declaring it finished, and finished means exposed to judgment.

Exhaustion. Maintaining impossible standards is exhausting. Every task takes more time and energy than it needs to because "good enough" isn't in your vocabulary. You're working harder than everyone around you and somehow still feeling like you're not doing enough.

Anxiety and depression. Research consistently links perfectionism to mental health struggles. When you're constantly falling short of impossible standards, you're constantly generating feelings of failure, inadequacy, and shame. It's a recipe for anxiety and depression.

Relationship strain. Here's the part that's hardest to admit: Perfectionism doesn't just affect you. It bleeds onto the people around you. The impossible standards you hold for yourself often become impossible standards for your partner, your children, and your colleagues. You might not mean to be critical, but when anything less than perfect feels intolerable, that intolerance shows.

Your children feel it when their homework isn't quite right, and you can't resist fixing it. Your partner feels it when nothing they do is quite enough. Your colleagues feel it when every project requires endless revisions to meet your standards.

Perfectionism isolates us. It makes us hard to please and hard to be around. It creates distance where we're longing for connection.

The Perfect Storm of Modern Life

Personal history isn't the only source of perfectionism. Our culture creates and reinforces it constantly.

Social media has made this exponentially worse. We're bombarded daily with images of perfect homes, perfect bodies, perfect families, and perfect lives. We know intellectually that these images are curated, filtered, and often faked—but emotionally, they still land. They still make us feel that everyone else has figured out something we haven't.

The comparison trap is relentless. Whatever you're doing, someone online is doing it better. Whatever you look like, someone looks more polished. Whatever your children achieve, someone else's children are achieving more. It's an endless treadmill of inadequacy.

And here's something I've observed: much of this pressure comes from other women.

That's a painful thing to name. We want to believe in sisterhood, in women supporting women. And that does exist. But so does the judgment, the competition, and the side-eye at the school gates when someone's child is struggling, or someone's appearance doesn't measure up, or someone's life is visibly imperfect.

Women can be brutal to each other about mothering choices, about work choices, about bodies and clothes and homes. The "mommy wars" are real. The judgment about whether you work or stay home, breastfeed or don't, have a spotless house or a lived-in one—it comes from other women as much as anywhere else.

This isn't about blaming women for each other's perfectionism. We're all caught in the same system, all wounded by the same impossible standards. Hurt people hurt people. Women who feel inadequate often cope by finding others to feel superior to.

But naming it matters. Because healing means recognizing all the sources of pressure—external as well as internal—and consciously choosing to opt out.

The Myth of the Perfect Mother

Nowhere is perfectionism more painful—or more futile—than in motherhood.

The standard for mothers is impossibly high. You should be patient but firm, nurturing but not smothering, and involved but not helicoptering. Your children should be well-behaved, well-adjusted, well-educated, and well-rounded. Your home should be clean and organized. You should work (but not too much) or stay home (but not just be a stay-at-home mom). You should be sexy for your partner but modest in public, ambitious but not neglectful, and present but not losing yourself.

It's impossible. All of it. No one has ever achieved it because it doesn't exist. The perfect mother is a myth—and chasing her is making real mothers miserable.

What children actually need is not perfection. They need presence. They need good enough. They need a mother who is human, who makes mistakes, who apologizes when she's wrong, and who shows them that imperfect people can still be loving and worthy and whole.

In fact, the psychoanalyst Donald Winnicott coined the term "good enough mother" specifically to release women from this impossible standard. His research showed that children don't need perfect parenting—they need adequate parenting. They actually benefit from minor failures and frustrations because these teach them that the world is survivable. That disappointment can be weathered. That they're capable of coping.

A perfect mother—if one existed—would actually harm her children by never allowing them to develop resilience.

So the perfectionism that tells you you're not doing enough, not being enough, and failing your children in a thousand small ways? It's not only wrong, it's also backward. Your imperfection is part of what your children need.

SHE CRIED TOO

Anne Lamott

"Perfectionism is the voice of the oppressor, the enemy of the people. It will keep you cramped and insane your whole life."

Anne Lamott is a beloved author whose books on writing, faith, and life are filled with hard-won wisdom about imperfection. Her concept of the "shitty first draft"—giving yourself permission to write badly before revising—has freed countless people from perfectionist paralysis. She writes about her own struggles with perfectionism, alcoholism, single motherhood, and the relentless inner critic that told her she wasn't enough. Her work is a testament to the power of embracing messiness—of starting before you're ready, finishing before it's perfect, and offering your imperfect gifts to the world anyway.

Done Is Better Than Perfect

Here's a phrase I want you to sit with:

Done is better than perfect.

I know. If you're a perfectionist, something in you recoils at this. Done but imperfect? That's failure. That's mediocrity. That's not good enough.

But think about it differently. A finished project that's 80 percent of your ideal is infinitely more valuable than a perfect project that never gets completed. A good-enough dinner that gets on the table is better than a gourmet meal that stresses you to tears. A functional, loving home is better than a spotless one where everyone's walking on eggshells.

Perfect is the enemy of done. And done is what actually moves your life forward.

I think about my first book sometimes. I wrote it years ago, with the knowledge and skills I had at the time. Looking back now, I can see all the ways I've grown and all the things I'd do differently. Part of me wishes I could contact everyone who read it and say, "I got better!"

But here's the thing: that book helped people. It reached readers who needed it when they needed it. If I'd waited until I was a better writer, until I knew more, until it was perfect—it never would have existed. The people it helped would have been left without it.

We can only do what we can do in this moment. The imperfect action taken today is worth more than the perfect action perpetually postponed.

Done is better than perfect. Start saying it to yourself. It might become a quiet revolution.

What You Model Matters

If you have children, there's another reason to work on your perfectionism: they're watching.

Children don't learn from what we say. They learn from what we do. If you're modeling relentless self-criticism, impossible standards, and the belief that nothing is ever good enough—that's what they'll learn. Not from your words about being kind to yourself, but from watching you be unkind to yourself every day.

I made a conscious choice with my own daughters. I told them that having a high IQ or any other talent is no different from having blue eyes or green. It's something you're born with. It doesn't make you better or worse than anyone else. It's simply part of who you are.

My youngest daughter, Samantha, is a high achiever in the commercial world. She succeeds, and she knows her success is partly a blessing, partly effort, and not a measure of her worth compared to anyone else. Humility in success is important. Excellence without arrogance. Achievement without needing to diminish others.

My oldest daughter, Katie, is brilliant in different ways—incredibly determined, equally capable, and equally aware that her abilities are gifts to be used, not badges of superiority.

I wanted to break the cycle I grew up with. The one that punished excellence, that made achievement shameful, that taught me to dim my light to avoid criticism. I wanted my girls to shine fully, without apology, while staying humble and kind.

And I wanted them to know that my love wasn't conditional on their performance. That they were enough—exactly as they were—before they achieved anything at all.

What do you want to model for the people watching you?

Embracing Good Enough

Letting go of "perfect" doesn't mean settling for mediocrity. It doesn't mean not caring about quality, or not trying your best, or lowering your standards to the floor.

It means recognizing the point of diminishing returns, where more effort doesn't produce meaningfully better results, just exhaustion and anxiety.

It means accepting that you are human, and humans make mistakes, and that's not just inevitable but okay.

It means defining success by your own values rather than by impossible external standards. What actually matters to you? Not what you think should matter, not what society says should matter, but what genuinely does?

It means celebrating completion. Finishing something is an achievement, even if—especially if—it's not perfect. The world is full of brilliant unfinished projects. Don't let yours be among them.

And it means extending to yourself the grace you'd extend to others. If your best friend did something imperfectly, would you berate her? If your child made a mistake, would you tell them they weren't good enough? Then why do you speak to yourself that way?

Good enough is not mediocre. Good enough is sustainable. Good enough is human. Good enough is *enough.*

A GENTLE INVITATION

Releasing Perfect

Consider these questions:

Where did you learn that you had to be perfect? What messages did you receive?

What is perfectionism protecting you from? What do you fear would happen if you weren't perfect?

What is perfectionism costing you? What are you missing because of it?

Where in your life could "good enough" be enough? What would you attempt if you didn't have to do it perfectly?

Choose one area this week to consciously practice "good enough." Notice what happens—both the discomfort and the freedom.

Perfectionism promises protection but delivers prison. It promises that if we just get it right, we'll finally be safe, accepted, and enough. But the goalposts keep moving. Perfect is always just out of reach. And we exhaust ourselves chasing something that doesn't exist.

Letting go of perfect is terrifying. It means accepting vulnerability, accepting that we can be criticized, accepting that we're human and flawed, and sometimes we'll get it wrong.

But it also means freedom. Freedom to start before you're ready. Freedom to finish before it's flawless. Freedom to try things that might not work. Freedom to live a full, imperfect, gloriously human life.

You don't have to earn your worth through perfection. You don't have to calibrate your achievements to avoid criticism. You don't have to walk that impossible tightrope anymore.

You can just... be. Imperfect and enough. Flawed and worthy. Human.

That's not settling. That's liberation.

Chapter Thirteen

The Long Game

John Lennon once wrote, "Life is what happens when you're busy making other plans."

He was right. Life doesn't wait for us to be ready. It arrives—sometimes gently, sometimes as a wrecking ball—regardless of our schedules, our ambitions, or our carefully constructed plans.

This book has been about surviving the wrecking ball moments. The overwhelm. The crying in the shower. The seasons when all you can do is get through the next hour, the next day, sometimes the next minute.

But survival mode isn't meant to be permanent. It's meant to be a temporary state that gets you through a crisis—not a way of life.

This chapter is about the long game. About shifting from constant crisis management to something more sustainable. About building a life that doesn't require you to run on empty, white-knuckle your way through each day, or collapse in tears behind locked doors.

It's about holding two truths at once—sometimes life demands our complete presence in the immediate moment, and sometimes we need to lift our eyes to the horizon and build toward something better.

The art is knowing which one this moment requires.

When Life Demands Everything

Years ago, I lost my husband, Clive, to lung cancer.

It happened so fast. One day, he noticed a "funny feeling" in his chest. The next day, doctors found a tumor in his lung—four centimeters, already aggressive. That was at the end of July. He died on the first of November, the same year.

Three months. From an odd sensation to gone.

In those weeks, I dropped everything. I had contracts I'd committed to, offices I ran, and staff who depended on me for their salaries. I shut it all down. Every bit of it.

Because in that moment, nothing else mattered. Not my career, not my obligations, not my carefully built professional life. What mattered was being present for Clive. Supporting him through his fear. Caring for him through the pain that grew worse each day. Being entirely, completely there.

Day by day. Hour by hour. Sometimes minute by minute.

He passed sooner than expected. But for those few weeks, he had my complete attention and commitment. I have never regretted that choice.

That's what some seasons require: everything. Your whole self, focused on what's right in front of you. No long-term planning, no strategy, no thinking about tomorrow. Just this moment, this breath, this person who needs you now.

If you're in a season like that—caring for a dying loved one, navigating a health crisis, surviving a trauma, managing an emergency—please hear me: It's okay to let everything else go. It's okay to shrink your world down to what's essential. It's okay to operate in survival mode.

That's not failure. That's wisdom.

When Survival Mode Becomes a Lifestyle

The problem comes when survival mode doesn't end.

After Clive passed, my world gradually reopened. I got back to work. Life continued, as it does, carrying me forward whether I felt ready or not.

But I've seen many women who get stuck in survival mode long after the crisis has passed. The emergency is over, but their nervous system doesn't know it. They're still operating as if every day is a fight for survival, even when the immediate threat has lifted.

And I've seen women whose lives have become a series of overlapping crises—one emergency bleeding into the next, never a moment to catch their breath. For them, survival mode isn't temporary. It's just... life.

If this is you, I want to gently suggest: this isn't sustainable. Humans aren't designed to live in constant crisis. Our bodies, our minds, our spirits—they need seasons of rest, of rebuilding, of playing the long game. Perpetual survival mode will break you eventually.

The question is, are you in genuine crisis right now, or have you become so accustomed to crisis mode that you've forgotten there's another way to live?

Sometimes the bravest thing is to acknowledge that the emergency is over and begin—

tentatively, gently—to build something sustainable.

SHE CRIED TOO

Emma Thompson

"You can't be brave if you've only had wonderful things happen to you."

Emma Thompson, the Oscar-winning actor and writer, has spoken openly about periods of deep exhaustion and depression throughout her career. After years of intense professional pressure and personal heartbreak, she described reaching a point where she had to step back and rebuild her life more deliberately. Thompson has often spoken about the importance of pacing oneself in a demanding world and recognizing that strength sometimes means slowing down rather than pushing harder. Her reflections remind us that resilience isn't about endless endurance—it's about learning how to live sustainably through both joy and difficulty.

The Art of Pacing

Long-term thinking and short-term survival aren't opposites. They're dance partners.

When you're in acute stress, you need to focus on the immediate: getting through this hour, this day. Long-term planning feels impossible and probably is—your brain literally can't access its strategic functions when it's flooded with stress hormones.

But even in crisis, small moments of lifting your eyes to the horizon can help. Reminding yourself: *This will pass. I won't feel this way forever. There is a future beyond this moment.*

This is where those techniques from earlier chapters become vital. The micro-moments that regulate your nervous system. The visualization of your future self who has already made it through. The brief timeouts that let you catch your breath before diving back in.

Pacing yourself in a crisis means:

Taking it in whatever increments you can manage. If you can't think about the whole week, think about today. If today is too much, think about this hour. If this hour is too much, think about the next five minutes. Shrink the timeframe until it becomes manageable.

Building in tiny recoveries. Even in the most demanding seasons, you need moments of rest. Not because you've earned them, but because you can't sustain the pace without them.

Keeping one eye on "after." Not in a way that takes you out of the present, but in a way that reminds you: this season will end. There will be an after. You're not just surviving; you're surviving *toward* something.

Knowing when to shift gears. The skill is recognizing when the acute phase is ending, and it's time to start rebuilding. This isn't always obvious. Sometimes we stay in crisis mode from habit, long after we could have started playing the long game again.

Small Changes, Big Impact

When it comes to building something sustainable, many women make the same mistake—they try to change everything at once.

It makes sense. When you finally lift your head from survival mode and see how far your life has drifted from what you want, the urge is to overhaul everything immediately. New routines, new boundaries, new habits, new everything. A complete life makeover, starting Monday.

This almost never works. It's too much, too fast. You're already depleted, and dramatic change takes enormous energy. Within weeks—sometimes days—the new regime collapses, and you're left feeling like a failure on top of everything else.

The long game is played differently. It's played with small, sustainable changes that compound over time.

One boundary, held consistently. One healthy habit, practiced until it's automatic. One small shift in how you structure your days. Then another. Then another.

This feels frustratingly slow when you're eager for change. But consider the mathematics: a tiny improvement, sustained over months and years, adds up to transformation. A dramatic improvement that lasts two weeks adds up to nothing.

Think about it this way: If you could be just 1 percent better at protecting your energy, 1 percent better at saying no, and 1 percent better at prioritizing rest—and you maintained that improvement consistently—where would you be in a year? In five years?

The long game isn't glamorous. It doesn't make for dramatic before-and-after stories. But it's what actually works.

Honoring the Seasons

Life moves in seasons, and wisdom lies in recognizing which season you're in.

There are seasons of planting—when you're building something new, investing energy in projects or relationships or dreams that won't bear fruit for a while.

There are seasons of growing—when things are developing, taking shape, requiring tending and patience.

There are seasons of harvest—when the work pays off, when you reap what you've sown, when abundance flows.

And there are seasons of rest—when the fields lie fallow, when nothing seems to be happening, when the only task is to wait and recover.

Our culture doesn't honor all these seasons equally. We celebrate planting and harvesting, but have little patience for growing or resting. We want constant productivity, constant forward motion, and constant results.

But trying to harvest when it's time to plant leads to frustration. Trying to plant when you need to rest leads to burnout. Fighting against the natural rhythm of your life exhausts you in ways that working with it never would.

What season are you in right now?

If you're in a season of survival—a new baby, an illness, a crisis, a loss—honor that. Don't expect yourself to be planting or harvesting. Just survive. That's enough.

If you're in a season of rest—recovering from burnout, healing from trauma, regathering your strength—honor that too. Don't let anyone make you feel lazy or unproductive. Rest is its own work.

And if the crisis has passed and you sense it might be time to start building again—honor that call. Don't stay in survival mode from habit. Begin, gently, to look toward the horizon again.

SHE CRIED TOO

Elizabeth Vargas

"I had to stop running long enough to figure out why I was running in the first place. Recovery isn't just about stopping the destructive behavior—it's about building a life you don't need to escape from."

Elizabeth Vargas was a star news anchor at ABC when she publicly revealed her battle with anxiety and alcohol addiction. For years, she'd powered through—high-functioning, successful, hiding her struggles behind professional competence. Her breakdown forced her to stop running and start rebuilding. In recovery, she didn't just address the addiction; she rebuilt her entire life—her relationships, her priorities, her way of being in the world. She learned that the goal isn't just to survive but to create a life sustainable enough that you don't need to numb yourself to get through it. Her book *Between Breaths* chronicles the hard work of playing the long game after hitting bottom.

The Life You're Building

Here's the real question the long game asks: What kind of life are you building?

Not what kind of life are you surviving. Not what kind of life are you enduring. What kind of life are you *building*?

Because every day, whether you're conscious of it or not, you're constructing something. Your habits are building a life. Your choices are building a life. The things you say yes to and no to are building a life.

The question is whether you're building intentionally or by default.

When you operate in pure survival mode, you build by default. You react to whatever's most urgent. You say yes to whatever's demanded. You let circumstances dictate the shape of your days, your weeks, and your years.

When you play the long game, you build intentionally. You make choices aligned with what you actually want your life to look like. You protect time and energy for what matters. You say no to things that aren't part of what you're building, even when they're good things, even when they're expected.

This doesn't mean controlling everything. Life will still throw curveballs. Plans will still be disrupted. Some seasons will still require pure survival.

But between the crises, in the ordinary days, you have more agency than you might think. You can shape the life you're building. You can make choices that move you toward something rather than just away from something.

What do you want your life to look like in five years? In ten? Not in detail—life doesn't work that way—but in broad strokes. What do you want to feel like? What do you want to have? Who do you want to be?

And what would you need to start doing now—or stop doing—to move in that direction?

Holding the Vision

Remember the future self-visualization from Chapter Eight? That technique isn't just for getting through crises. It's also for playing the long game.

Your future self—the woman who has built something sustainable, who has created a life that doesn't require constant crisis management, who has found her way to the other side of overwhelm—she's real. She exists in potential. Every choice you make either moves you toward her or away from her.

Keeping her in mind helps when the short term is hard. When you're tempted to abandon a healthy boundary because it's causing conflict. When you're exhausted and the sustainable choice takes more energy than the depleting one. When the long game feels too long, and you want results now.

She's waiting for you. The you who rested enough to have energy. The you who said no enough to have space. The you who built something that nourishes rather than drains.

What would she want you to choose today?

A GENTLE INVITATION

Playing Your Long Game

Take some time with these questions:

What season are you in right now? Is it time to survive, to rest, to plant, or to build?

Are you stuck in survival mode even though the crisis has passed? What would it mean to start building again?

What is one small, sustainable change you could make that would compound over time?

What kind of life are you building by default? What kind would you build if you were intentional?

Picture yourself five years from now, living sustainably. What does she want you to know?

Life will keep happening while you're busy making other plans. There will be more crises, more seasons of survival, and more moments when all you can do is breathe through the next hour.

But there will also be spaces between the crises. Ordinary days. Moments of calm. And in those spaces, you have a choice: stay in survival mode from habit, or begin building something sustainable.

The long game isn't about having a perfect five-year plan. It's not about controlling the uncontrollable or predicting the unpredictable. It's simply about making choices today that your future self will thank you for.

Small changes, sustained over time. Boundaries held consistently. Rest taken regularly. One percent better, again and again.

You're not just surviving. You're building.

Build something that doesn't require tears behind locked doors. Build something that lets you breathe. Build something that your future self—the one waiting for you on the other side of this season—would recognize as a life worth living.

That's the long game. And it's the only one worth playing.

Chapter Fourteen

Stepping Out of the Shower

You've come so far.

When you picked up this book, perhaps you were that woman behind the locked bathroom door. Water running to mask the sound of your sobs. Holding yourself together for everyone else, falling apart in the only private space you had. Wondering if anyone understood. Wondering if it would ever get better. Wondering if there was something wrong with you for feeling so overwhelmed when everyone else seemed to be managing just fine.

Now, fourteen chapters later, you know the truth: you're not alone. You never were.

You've learned about the weight you carry—visible and invisible, physical and emotional. You've understood where it came from, how the stories you inherited shaped the woman you became. You've seen what chronic overwhelm does to your body and why self-care isn't selfish but essential.

You've gathered tools—micro-moments that can shift your state in seconds and deeper practices that reclaim your mind from chaos. You've learned about boundaries, about rest, and about letting go of perfect. You've met women who've walked this path before you, who've cried these same tears, who've found their way through.

And perhaps most importantly, you've given yourself permission. Permission to struggle. Permission to need help. Permission to be human.

That's no small thing.

This Is Not a Destination

I want to be honest with you as we reach the end: Reading this book hasn't "fixed" you.

Not because the book failed, and not because you failed. But because there's no finish line. No moment where you arrive at "healed" and never struggle again. No magical transformation that makes you immune to overwhelm forever.

There will be hard days ahead. Days when the old patterns pull at you, when the weight feels crushing again, when you find yourself back behind that bathroom door with tears streaming down your face.

This is not failure. This is life.

The difference is that now you have tools. Now you understand what's happening in your body and your mind when overwhelm hits. Now you know you're not alone, not broken, not uniquely incapable of handling what other women handle with ease.

Now you can meet the hard moments differently.

This isn't a destination. It's a practice. Something you'll return to again and again, imperfectly, for the rest of your life. Some seasons you'll do it well; others you'll forget everything you've learned and have to start again. That's okay. That's how it works.

The goal isn't perfection. The goal is returning—always returning—to the practices that support you, the boundaries that protect you, and the truth that you are worthy of care.

What I Hope You Remember

If you remember nothing else from this book, I hope you remember this:

You are precious and perfect, exactly as you are.

Not when you lose the weight. Not when you get the promotion. Not when your house is clean, your children are thriving, your marriage is harmonious, and your life looks like the highlight reel you see on other people's social media.

Now. Today. In your mess, your struggle, your imperfection.

You are enough. You have always been enough. The voice that tells you otherwise is lying.

And I hope you remember this, too: **You can do this.** Whatever "this" is—the challenge you're facing, the life you're building, the healing you're undertaking—you can do it.

But perhaps on your terms. Not the world's terms. Not the terms of everyone around you who has opinions about how you should live, what you should want, and who you should be.

Your terms. Based on *your* values. Honoring *your* limits. Building *your* life.

You get to decide what that looks like. You get to define what success means for you. You get to choose which voices you listen to and which expectations you refuse.

That's not selfish. That's sovereignty. And it's your birthright.

The Woman You're Becoming

Throughout this book, I've invited you to imagine your future self—the woman who has navigated through this season, who has built something sustainable, and who has found her way to the other side of overwhelm.

She's not a fantasy. She's a possibility. And every choice you make either moves you toward her or away from her.

She's not perfect. She's still human, still struggling with some things, still learning. But she's different from where you are now. She's rested more. She's protected her boundaries. She's stopped trying to earn her worth through exhaustion. She's learned to receive care as well as give it.

She still cries sometimes. But not because she's broken. Because she's human, and humans cry. And she doesn't have to hide it in the shower anymore because she's not pretending to be okay. She's allowed herself to be real.

She's waiting for you. And she's proud of how far you've already come.

Stepping Out

The shower has been a place of tears. A place of hiding. The only space where you could let the mask fall and feel what you were actually feeling.

But it's time to step out.

Not because you're fixed. Not because you'll never need to cry again. But because you don't have to hide anymore.

You can be overwhelmed *and* supported. You can be struggling *and* held. You can be imperfect *and* loved.

The world outside the bathroom door hasn't changed. It's still demanding, still chaotic, still full of people who need things from you. But you've changed. You have tools now. You have understanding. You have permission to take care of yourself.

So dry your tears. Turn off the water. Unlock the door.

Step out into your life—not the life that's expected of you but the one you're choosing to build. One small change at a time. One boundary at a time. One breath at a time.

You can do this.

And you don't have to do it alone.

SHE CRIED TOO

Jill—The Woman Who Wrote This Book

"When I found myself ugly-crying in the shower, I didn't know it would become a book. I just knew I was drowning. Writing this—for you—became a lifeline for me too."

I need you to know something: I didn't write this book from a place of having it all figured out. I wrote it from the shower floor. I wrote it while navigating my husband's dementia, while rebuilding my life in a new country, while carrying fears and losses and challenges I haven't fully shared in these pages. I wrote it because I needed it as much as you did. And something unexpected happened: the writing healed me. Focusing on what might help you helped me. This book became a tool for others and a reminder for me—that we're all in this together, that none of us has to carry it alone, that even the woman writing the book about overwhelm is sometimes overwhelmed. I'm her too. I've always been her too. And that's exactly why I understand.

A GENTLE INVITATION

Your First Step Out

Before you close this book, choose one thing:

One tool from these pages that you'll use this week.

One boundary you'll hold.

One way you'll rest.

One moment of permission you'll give yourself.

Just one. Write it down. Commit to it. Let it be the first small step into your new chapter.

Then take another step. And another. One at a time, for as long as it takes.

Thank you for trusting me with your tears.

Thank you for reading these pages, for doing the hard work of looking honestly at your life, and for believing that something could be different.

It can be. It will be. Not perfectly, not easily, but really.

You are precious. You are worthy. You are enough.

Now step out of the shower, my friend.

Your life is waiting.

Here is the complete Letter to You, with both workbook references woven in, ready to copy and paste:

A Letter to You

Dear Reader,

If you've made it this far, I want you to know something: I'm proud of you.

Not because reading this book is a great achievement — but because opening it took courage. It meant admitting something wasn't working. It meant being willing to look honestly at your life. It meant believing, even tentatively, that change was possible.

That takes bravery. Especially when you're exhausted.

I want you to know that I wrote every word of this book with you in mind. Not an abstract reader, but you — the specific woman holding these pages, with your specific struggles and your specific tears and your specific hopes for something better.

I don't know your name. I don't know the details of what brought you here. But I know the feeling that drove you to pick up a book called *Crying in the Shower.* I know it because I've felt it too.

We're connected now, you and I. Through these pages, through shared experience, through the universal truth that being a woman in this world can be beautiful and brutal in equal measure.

Here's what I want to leave you with:

You are not too much. Your needs are not too much. Your feelings are not too much. The help you require is not too much. Anyone who has made you feel otherwise was wrong.

You are not too little. You are not inadequate, insufficient, or incapable. You are a human being doing the best you can with what you have. That's all any of us can do.

You are allowed to take up space. In your own life. In your own story. You don't have to shrink yourself to make others comfortable. You don't have to diminish your needs to avoid being a burden. You are allowed to exist fully, completely, unapologetically.

The journey from here isn't straight. There will be setbacks and hard days and moments when you forget everything you've learned. That's okay. Just keep coming back. Keep returning to the truth of who you are. Keep choosing yourself, again and again.

Before you go, I want to give you something. I've created a free companion workbook — *Wrapping Up Warm: A Companion Workbook to Crying in the Shower* — where every exercise, reflection, and gentle invitation in this book is gathered in one place, ready for you to work through in your own time. No catch, no sign-up hoops, no cost. Just tools, because you deserve them. Download it free at www.bighornwellness.com.

You already know someone who needs this book. You probably thought of her name somewhere around Chapter Two. Pass it on when you're ready — leave it on her doorstep, slip it into her bag, send it with a text that just says "this made me think of you."

That's how we help each other. Quietly, without fanfare, one woman at a time.

And if it helped you — if something in these pages made you feel a little less alone — I'd be so grateful if you'd take two minutes to leave a review wherever you bought it. Not for me. For the woman who's standing in her shower right now, wondering if anyone understands. Your words might be the thing that convinces her to pick it up.

And on the days when you find yourself back in that shower, water running, tears falling — remember that you're not alone. Remember that somewhere out there, I'm thinking of you. Remember that this, too, shall pass.

Remember that you can do this.

With all my heart,

Jill

Who cried too, and found her way through

Appendix

A Beginner's Guide to Self-Hypnosis

Throughout this book, I've mentioned self-hypnosis as one of the most powerful tools in my personal and professional tool kit. Now it's time to teach you how to do it yourself.

This appendix will give you everything you need to begin practicing self-hypnosis safely and effectively. It's designed for complete beginners—you don't need any prior experience or special abilities. If you can daydream, you can learn self-hypnosis.

I've also included a script you can record on your phone and play back to yourself. Many people find this helpful when starting out, as it allows you to fully relax without having to remember what comes next.

While self-hypnosis is a wonderful skill for managing everyday stress, building resilience, and supporting your well-being, I also want to encourage you to consider working with a qualified Hypnotist if you're dealing with deeper issues. A professional can tailor sessions to your specific needs and guide you through more complex work. Self-hypnosis is a complement to professional support, not necessarily a replacement for it.

For additional free resources, including guided audio recordings, please visit my website at **www.bighornwellness.com**.

What Self-Hypnosis Actually Is

Let's start by clearing up some misconceptions.

Self-hypnosis is not:

- Mind control or manipulation
- Being unconscious or asleep
- Giving up control of your mind
- Something that only works on certain people
- Dangerous or scary
- Self-hypnosis IS:
- A natural state of focused attention
- A state of deep relaxation combined with heightened inner awareness
- A way of communicating with your subconscious mind
- A learnable skill that improves with practice
- Completely safe when practiced appropriately

You've already experienced hypnotic states many times in your life. When you're so absorbed in a book or film that you lose track of time. When you drive a familiar route and arrive without remembering the journey. When you daydream so vividly that you feel emotion from the imagined scenario. These are all naturally occurring trance states.

Self-hypnosis simply means learning to enter this state deliberately and using it for your own benefit.

What Self-Hypnosis Can Help With

Regular self-hypnosis practice can support you with:

Stress and anxiety reduction — calming your nervous system and creating a sense of inner peace.

Sleep improvement — releasing the tension that keeps you awake and preparing your mind for rest.

Confidence building — reinforcing positive beliefs about yourself and your capabilities.

Emotional regulation — creating space between stimulus and response.

Pain management — changing your perception of and relationship with physical discomfort.

Breaking unwanted habits — accessing the subconscious patterns that drive automatic behaviors.

Enhancing performance — mentally rehearsing success in any area of life.

Processing emotions — creating a safe space to feel and release what you've been carrying.

Before You Begin

Choose your space. Find somewhere quiet where you won't be disturbed. This could be a bedroom, a comfortable chair, or even your parked car. The key is privacy and minimal interruptions.

Choose your position. You can practice self-hypnosis sitting or lying down. If you tend to fall asleep easily, sitting is better. Make sure you're comfortable but not so comfortable that sleep is inevitable.

Set a time. Decide how long you want to practice. For beginners, 10–15 minutes is plenty. You can set a gentle alarm if you're worried about time, though with practice you'll develop an internal sense of when to emerge.

Remove distractions. Silence your phone. Let household members know not to disturb you. Handle any physical needs (bathroom, water, temperature) before you begin.

Set an intention. Before each session, know what you want to focus on. This might be general relaxation, a specific suggestion you want to give yourself, or a feeling you want to cultivate.

> **TIP**
>
> You can record the following script on your phone and play it back to yourself. Read slowly with pauses between sentences. Your own voice is particularly effective because your subconscious mind recognizes and trusts it.

The Five Steps of Self-Hypnosis

Self-hypnosis follows a simple structure:

1. **Induction** — Guiding yourself into a relaxed, focused state.

2. **Deepening** — Taking that relaxation deeper.

3. **Suggestion** — Giving yourself the positive messages or imagery you want to absorb.

4. **Future pacing** — Imagining yourself using these new resources in your daily life.

5. **Emerging** — Returning to full waking awareness, feeling refreshed.

Let me walk you through each step.

Step 1: Induction

The induction is how you transition from ordinary waking consciousness into a hypnotic state. There are many techniques;

I'll teach you a simple, effective method combining eye fixation with progressive relaxation.

Begin by fixing your eyes on a spot slightly above your natural eyeline—this could be a point on the ceiling, on the wall, or simply imagined. Focusing your eyes upward naturally triggers the beginning of a trance state.

As you hold your gaze, allow your breathing to slow and deepen. Don't force it—just let each breath become a little slower, a little deeper than the one before.

Notice that as you continue to focus, your eyelids begin to feel heavy. This is natural. When they feel too heavy to keep open, simply let them close. This closing of the eyes is your signal to yourself that you're entering a relaxed state.

With your eyes closed, begin a progressive relaxation. Bring your attention to the top of your head, and imagine a wave of relaxation beginning there. Let it flow down over your forehead, releasing tension. Down over your eyes, your cheeks, your jaw. Let your jaw soften and relax. Down through your neck and shoulders, where so many of us hold tension. Let your shoulders drop. Down through your arms to your fingertips. Through your chest and back. Through your belly, letting it soften. Through your hips, your thighs, your knees, your calves, all the way down to your feet and toes.

Take your time with this. There's no rush.

Step 2: Deepening

Once you're relaxed, you can deepen the state. A simple and effective technique is the staircase method.

Imagine yourself at the top of a beautiful staircase with ten steps leading down. With each step you descend, you'll go deeper into relaxation.

Step 10... taking the first step down, feeling yourself relax a little more.

Step 9... deeper and more comfortable.

Step 8... letting go of any remaining tension.

Step 7... calm and peaceful.

Step 6... halfway down now, deeply relaxed.

Step 5... going deeper still.

Step 4... so comfortable, so at ease.

Step 3... almost there.

Step 2... one more step.

Step 1... at the bottom now, deeply, comfortably relaxed.

At the bottom of the stairs, you might imagine a peaceful place—a garden, a beach, a cozy room, anywhere that feels safe and calm to you. This is your inner sanctuary, a place you can return to whenever you need peace.

Step 3: Suggestion

This is the heart of self-hypnosis—the moment when you give yourself the positive messages you want your subconscious mind to absorb.

Suggestions work best when they are:

Positive — Focus on what you want, not what you don't want. "I am calm and confident" rather than "I am not anxious."

Present tense — Phrase suggestions as if they're already true. "I am" rather than "I will be."

Personal — Use "I" statements. Make them about you.

Believable — Your subconscious will resist suggestions that feel completely impossible. Start with suggestions that stretch but don't snap your belief.

Specific — The more specific, the more powerful. "I speak confidently in meetings" is stronger than "I am confident."

Some examples of effective suggestions:

I am calm and centered, even in challenging situations.

I trust myself to handle whatever comes.

I deserve rest, and I allow myself to receive it.

I release what I cannot control.

I am enough, exactly as I am.

My boundaries protect me, and I hold them with ease.

Repeat your chosen suggestions several times, slowly. Let them sink in. Imagine them being absorbed by your subconscious mind like water soaking into soil.

Step 4: Future Pacing

Future pacing means imagining yourself in future situations, using the resources you're building. This helps bridge the gap between the hypnotic state and real life.

Think of a situation where you want to feel or behave differently. Maybe it's a stressful meeting, a difficult conversation, or a moment when you typically lose your calm.

Now imagine yourself in that situation, but different. See yourself responding with the calm, the confidence, and the boundaries you've been suggesting. Make it vivid—see what you'd see, hear what you'd hear, and feel what you'd feel. Notice how good it feels to respond this way.

This mental rehearsal primes your brain to respond this way when the real situation arises. You're creating a template for your future self to follow.

Step 5: Emerging

When you're ready to return to full waking awareness, do so gently and gradually. There's no rush.

You might count yourself up from 1 to 5:

1... beginning to return to full awareness.

2... becoming more aware of your body, your surroundings.

3... feeling refreshed and alert.

4... almost fully back now.

5... eyes open, fully awake, feeling wonderful.

Take a moment to orient yourself. Wiggle your fingers and toes. Take a few breaths. Notice how you feel.

You might feel deeply relaxed, energized, peaceful, or some combination. These feelings often linger after the session, which is one of the many benefits of regular practice.

A Complete Self-Hypnosis Script

Here is a complete script you can record and play back to yourself. Read it slowly, with natural pauses. Speak gently and soothingly—you're talking to yourself with kindness.

SCRIPT

Recording Script for Self-Hypnosis

[Begin recording]

Find a comfortable position and allow your eyes to focus on a spot slightly above your eye level. It might be a point on the ceiling, a place on the wall, or simply a spot you imagine in front of you.

As you hold your gaze there, allow your breathing to slow down naturally. There's nothing to force, nothing to make an effort about. Just let each breath become a little slower... a little deeper... than the one before.

And as you continue to focus, you might notice that your eyelids are beginning to feel heavy. That's perfectly natural. It's a sign that you're relaxing. And when they feel too heavy to keep open, simply let them close.

[Pause 10 seconds]

Good. With your eyes comfortably closed, I'd like you to imagine a wave of relaxation beginning at the very top of your head. Feel it flowing down over your forehead, smoothing away any tension. Down over your eyes, your cheeks, your jaw. Let your jaw soften and relax.

That wave of relaxation continues down through your neck... and into your shoulders. We hold so much tension in our shoulders. Just let them drop. Let them soften. Let them relax.

The relaxation flows down through your arms... through your elbows... your forearms... your wrists... your hands... all the way to your fingertips.

And back up now, that wave continues through your chest, letting your breathing become even more relaxed. Through your back, releasing any tension held there. Through your stomach, letting it soften completely.

Down through your hips... your thighs... your knees... your calves... your ankles... your feet... all the way to the tips of your toes. Your whole body now comfortable, relaxed, at ease.

[Pause 5 seconds]

Now imagine yourself at the top of a beautiful staircase. There are ten steps leading down, and with each step, you'll go deeper into this peaceful, relaxed state.

Step 10... taking the first step down, feeling yourself relax even more.

Step 9... deeper and more comfortable.

Step 8... letting go completely.

Step 7... calm and peaceful.

Step 6... halfway down now, so deeply relaxed.

Step 5... going deeper still.

Step 4... so comfortable, so at ease.

Step 3... almost there now.

Step 2... one more step.

Step 1... at the bottom now. Deeply, comfortably, peacefully relaxed.

[Pause 5 seconds]

At the bottom of the stairs, you find yourself in a peaceful place. This is your inner sanctuary—a place of complete safety, complete calm. Take a moment to notice what's here. What do you see? What do you hear? What do you feel? Let this place become vivid and real.

[Pause 10 seconds]

In this deep, relaxed state, your subconscious mind is open and receptive. And I'd like you to absorb these truths:

I am enough, exactly as I am.

[Pause]

I am calm and centered, even in challenging situations.

[Pause]

I trust myself to handle whatever comes.

[Pause]

I deserve rest, and I allow myself to receive it.

[Pause]

I release what I cannot control.

[Pause]

I am precious and worthy of care.

[Pause 5 seconds]

Now imagine a moment in your future—perhaps tomorrow, perhaps next week—when you might have felt stressed or overwhelmed. But this time, see yourself responding differently. See yourself calm, grounded, capable. Notice how you hold yourself. Notice how you breathe. Notice how it feels to respond from this place of inner strength.

[Pause 10 seconds]

Know that this calm, this capability, this strength—it's inside you. It's always been inside you. And you can access it whenever you need it.

In a moment, I'm going to count from 1 to 5, and with each number, you'll become more awake, more alert, more refreshed. By the time I reach 5, you'll be fully awake, feeling wonderful.

1... beginning to return now, bringing these good feelings with you.

2... becoming more aware of your body, your surroundings.

3... feeling refreshed, alert, peaceful.

4... almost fully back now, feeling wonderful.

5... eyes open, fully awake, feeling calm, refreshed, and ready for your day.

[End recording]

Tips for Successful Practice

Practice regularly. Like any skill, self-hypnosis improves with practice. Aim for daily practice, even if just for ten minutes. Consistency matters more than duration.

Be patient with yourself. Some people go deep quickly; others take longer to learn. There's no right way to experience hypnosis. Trust your own process.

Don't try too hard. Hypnosis is about allowing, not forcing. If you're trying really hard to relax, you're creating tension. Just let it happen.

Customize your suggestions. The suggestions in the script are general. Feel free to replace them with suggestions more specific to your needs and goals.

Keep a journal. Note what works for you, what insights arise, and how you feel after practice. This helps you refine your approach over time.

Consider professional guidance. If you're working on deeper issues—trauma, phobias, significant anxiety—please consider working with a qualified Hypnotist who can tailor sessions to your specific needs and provide professional support.

Self-hypnosis is a gift you give yourself—a way of accessing your own inner wisdom, calming your own nervous system, and programming your own mind for the life you want to live.

It takes practice. It takes patience. But once you have it, it's yours forever—a tool that can't be taken from you, that requires no equipment or expense, and that's available whenever you need it.

For additional resources, guided recordings, and information about working with me directly, please visit **www.bighornwellness.com**.

You have everything you need within you. Self-hypnosis simply helps you access it.

Bibliography

Doyle, G. *Untamed.* Diversified Publishing, 2020.

Gilbert, E. *Eat, pray, love: One woman's search for everything across Italy, India and Indonesia.* Bloomsbury, 2010.

Huffington, A. *Thrive: The third metric to redefining success and creating a life of well-being, wisdom, and wonder.* Harmony, 2015.

Nagoski, E. & Nagoski, A. *Burnout: The secret to unlocking the stress cycle.* Ballantine Books, 2020.

Rimes, S. *Year of yes: How to dance it out, stand in the sun and be your own person.* Scribner, 2016.

van der Kolk, B. *The body keeps the score: Brain, mind, and body in the healing of trauma.* Penguin Books, 2015.

Vargas, E. *Between breaths: A memoir of panic and addiction.* Grand Central Publishing, 2016.

AUTHOR BIO

Jill is a board-certified hypnosis instructor, board-certified hypnotist, MEMI practitioner, master relationship and family coach, and creator of the Harmony Protocol. With decades of experience in therapeutic practice, she has helped countless individuals and families navigate crisis, loss, and transformation.

Her expertise spans clinical hypnosis, life and wellness coaching, and teenage suicide prevention—an area where her work has made her a respected voice and advocate. She brings to her practice both rigorous professional training and the wisdom that comes from her own journey through widowhood, cancer survivorship, and the challenges of building a new life in a new country.

Originally from England, Jill lived across Europe before immigrating to the United States, where she became a citizen in 2023. She now lives in Kentucky with her husband and their small white schnauzer, Alfred, and goldendoodle, Bertie.

Crying in the Shower is her most personal book yet—written from the shower floor, for every woman who has hidden her tears and wondered if she was the only one struggling.

She is the author of several books and the founder of Bighorn Wellness. Visit www.bighornwellness.com for free resources, guided recordings, and information about working with Jill directly.

www.ingramcontent.com/pod-product-compliance
Lightning Source LLC
LaVergne TN
LVHW090601110826
845146LV00001B/212
* 9 7 9 8 9 9 1 6 6 9 9 3 1 *